MODERN BRITISH FOOD

Recipes from Parlour

Jesse
Dunford
Wood

A.

Dedicated to those close by my side every step of the way, Mrs Jesse, Ada and Monty, and to those that are missed, particularly Great Granny Angela, whose shortbread recipe on page 179 will live longer than any of us.

MODERN BRITISH FOOD

Contents

Introduction

Cooking has to be one of the most brilliant skills to have in life, regardless of whether you are a professional or not. It is an empowering gift, cookery; one that people often look up to and aspire to. It is a great skill that will also be a never-ending lesson of discovery.

Food can be fuel, but it can't help but give pleasure. It brings warmth, both physically and emotionally, to both those that yearn and crave it, but also to those who don't even know they need it. It brings joy and great excitement in celebration, and also offers comfort when you're feeling low or down. We love the nostalgic heart tweaks that food can bring, dishes that taste of times gone by, a mother's this or an old-fashioned that, memories of school dinners and scabby knees, past lovers, of times and places. It can bring strangers closer, and it so often bring families together. Food really is a healer, and no matter your opinion on it (and amazingly everyone does have one) it is something we all look forward to.

Growing up in an artistic family, food always seemed like such a great idea, another form of artistic expression, but it wasn't usually prioritised in our family and it too often got rather overlooked. We did have freshly baked bread (even if I did dream of sliced Mighty White at primary school), homemade jam and cakes at birthdays, but this is where my homemade family food memories really rather dry up. With all the buzzing creativity there was, food wasn't a hugely important part of the meal times, but being together, I think, was much more important.

It is an empowering gift, cookery...

Burnt crusts, slightly undercooked spaghetti and the overly runny jam was ignored with the friendly glint of a rather too relaxed attitude to what was actually being made.

Once I reached teenage-dom and went to boarding school, I then had three meals a day provided with military discipline, on the dot of 7.30am, 12.15pm and 5.45pm. It was regular, dependable, familiar, and I thought, usually delicious. But it was only once I left the safety and comfort of the school routine and had to go out into the real world and fend for myself that I ever thought about food; where it came from, and how it came to be. And what a shock that was.

I would sit at home alone in my early art-college days eating slightly undercooked spaghetti with a sauce made from tomato purée and

Grandpa Tom in 1956 at the Dorchester. Some might think cooking has been in our genes, but he is still to master the very basics, even now at the age of 87. This photo is from the *Daily Express*, when he was a budding reporter 'posing' as a masterchef.

rubbery supermarket value range bacon strips – far from the romantic and delicious Italian dish of smoked ham, fresh tomato sauce over some just-al dente papardelle that I might have been dreaming of. So I made a plan and a commitment to learn to cook, not be flustered by recipes of more than four ingredients (which too often is a common roadblock many people come up against) and stick to it. What is the worst that could happen?

I then learnt to cook.

I cooked food that my then-landlord (and Grandfather) didn't complain about. I cooked biscuits that I took into art school, that disappeared much too quickly; I cooked a nearly romantic meal of Bolognese (not really recommending as a courting dish) for my new girlfriend using too much of dear Grandpa's dry sherry; I ended up cooking (epic) dinners in the under-used dining room for the hungry hoards of student friends of mine, and loved the idea that I could set the scene with music, table decorations and lighting – ask people to dress up even – and then feed them food, drinks and have a brilliant time entertaining and hosting.

The seeds were then sown for the fantastically romantic idea of having an outrageously on-going-money-making-dinner-party, which some people might call a restaurant. I live that dream these days. And usually it is fun. Sometimes though, it is hard and tricky. Often it is heartwarmingly rewarding. Sometimes it is awkward and challenging, and occasionally we even make a little money. But I am living the reality of an independent host, and love all that comes with it.

When it comes to others though, I have found that people often fall into three camps when talking about cooking skills:

1. Those with none;
2. Those who are military conformists;
3. And then those free-spirited adventurer types that take an idea and run with it.

I am rather hoping that this book can offer advice, guidance and even inspiration to almost all of those people.

It is rare, but not uncommon, to find people who have got all the way to middle age, occasionally even surviving to old age, who have NO skills in the kitchen. Those who rely on the food of others; be them spouses, relatives, supermarkets and their pre-packed offerings, and also more often than not, restaurants. People who pride themselves on their boiled egg and toast reportoire. *This is my Grandfather.*

The other camp, the military conformists, are those who religiously stick to recipes that have been followed, down to the last ¼ teaspoon of the spice they have never heard of and bought especially. Those who never stray from the holy grail of the words that someone somewhere has put down for them. I find there is a brilliant lack of responsibility these cooks have towards their cooking, as someone else has done all the thinking for them, but then again an endearing trust. Blaming the author or the instruction for any failures, but on the other hand always taking the applause when it goes well. *This is my Father.*

> ## I have found that people often fall into three camps...

The adventurers might look at a picture, could even stretch to reading the recipes, but will rarely follow what is written. They will get the gist and do an interpretation of it, put a bit of themselves into the dish, by using 'pistachios instead because they are in the cupboard' or 'I used twice as much, as I didn't like the sound of what they suggested'. Those people! Those people will understand what they are doing sometimes because they have really thought about it and considered the consequences. It is cooking from the heart. *This is my Mother.*

This book is all about giving you direction and inspiration of course, but also to feed you ideas of what you could do with these dishes as a base, even offering you alternatives, little nudges of versions and off-piste adventures you could go on to make them your own.

There is nothing more satisfying, and I still feel it every day, than making something lovely and sharing it with others. We do it on an industrial scale professionally, which has its challenges but also benefits, but I still love cooking for my wife and kids when there was apparently nothing in the fridge worth salvaging.

little nudges of versions and off-piste adventures...

My food, in essence, is all about accessibility, but making it as interesting, rich and deep as you want it to be. Food should not be intimidating – basic cookery is pretty simple. There are some brilliant three step recipes here like the best scrambled eggs ever (page 55) with two ingredients that could even change what you think about scrambled eggs, and then there are other more long-winded affairs, which straddle more than one page, maybe even three, that may take days to prepare – start small and work towards those ones. You will get there in the end.

In essence our Cow Pie (see page 95) is just a meat pie, but there is a great steak and ale stew underneath that fantastic suet pastry that even tastes of cow – and a marrow bone chimney exploding out of the middle, laden with the marrow, mustard, parsley and breadcrumbs. It is a dish that can be made with other meats, other bases rather than beer, even other pastry – and this is a dish that will satisfy a dustman, a chef, a foodie and old man, perhaps even a young lady. It is delicious, good looking, humorous, confident, nostalgic and warming – it hits the spot on many levels and touches different people in different ways and satisfies the tummy, the mind, the heart and all those that eat it. I am very proud of this dish and the way it represents the food I believe in.

This book should help add a little extra to your cooking; might even delight you with the familiar yet unexpected, enrich your knowledge and know-how and give you a solid foundation from my rose-tinted view of Great British food.

Or if all else fails, skip all the other recipes and perhaps it will just show you how to make a wonderful pie.

Bottoms up!

mushroom 'tea'

tea 'cup

crumpets

mushroom and tarragon butter

Savoury

The Definition of a Salad
—now available without leaves

I n my first head chef's job, at the National Gallery, we got a lovely review from Guy Diamond of *Time Out* magazine who described it as 'British food, now available in colour!' I loved that – in fact I loved it so much I even suggested it as the title for this book.

British food doesn't have a great reputation around the world. That is a fact, less so an opinion. We are famous for fish and chips, bangers and mash, pie and liquor, spotted dick and lumpy custard. Often brown, normally stodgy, and rarely seasonal.

So I've had a think, funked things up a little...

Now think of all the beautiful things this country has to offer, even some of the delightful things in this simple book: the colour, the vibrancy, the variety. By using less well-known, but not unfamiliar ingredients in an interesting and creative way, there opens a whole other realm of cookery, a whole other pantry of possibilities. Take salads...

A 'British' salad is traditionally a split gem lettuce with a radish, cucumber and tomato, shrouded in an acidic blanket of salad cream. Not the lightest or healthiest of dishes, nor the most versatile or inspiring. So I have had a think, funked things up a little, and come up with some different salad ideas to help brighten up your life.

Salad doesn't always have to have an iceberg base, it doesn't even have to have a leaf in it. The *Oxford English Dictionary* (the one the whole world looks to for the definitive way) tells us that a salad is, by definition, 'A cold dish of various mixtures of raw or cooked vegetables, usually seasoned with oil, vinegar, or other dressing and sometimes accompanied by meat, fish, or other ingredients.'

So I have let go of the lettuce and salad leaf shackles, and added some serious crunch, colour and fun to the following recipes.

Let there be life!

Salad doesn't always have to
have an iceberg base...

Raw Vegetable 'Ravioli' with Goats' Cheese

Opening a restaurant in Italy, as I did a few years ago, you cannot help but be inspired by the brilliant food there, steeped in tradition and generations of knowledge. Our restaurant just happened to be in a clothes shop, with the kitchen in the changing room and washing up in the toilet hand sink. We had little equipment and no space, but we managed sixty customers a day, eight courses per person, and an awful lot of dishes flying out from behind the shrouded curtain.

It was a pop-up at a design fair, sadly only open for six days, desperately trying to help flog designer tables and chairs, and what better way to entice people to sit down and talk about the wonderful furniture than to feed them a 'quick' eight-course menu on the house. Great fun and high energy, too. It was my take on Italian food in an interesting and English way – or was it English food in an interesting and Italian way? I never could work that out.

This is the dish inspired by that trip. You really have to think of it as a goats' cheese salad; ravioli it is not, by any stretch, but with a little imagination you might just see the threads of likeness.

Served with a chopped sweet and sour vinaigrette of golden raisins, capers and cranberries (known as *agrodolce* in Italy): not a traditional dish by any means, but fun, slightly familiar, wonderfully delicious and fresh.

Serves 6

Raw Vegetables*

1 large beetroot
1 large golden beetroot
1 kohlrabi
1 swede
250ml white wine vinegar
150ml water
2 pinches of salt

*   in place of the vegetables used here, you could also use the golden or stripy (Chioggia) beetroot varieties, turnips, daikon or fancy large radishes you get in the season, butternut squash, courgette, cucumber or perhaps even lettuce or spinach leaves

RAW VEGETABLES / Peel and slice the vegetables very thinly using a mandoline, or failing that slice them very carefully and thinly with a knife. You could keep them in their natural sliced shape, or cut out shapes with a cookie cutter to make the pieces all the same size. You need two slices of each piece of veg per person – a total of eight slices per person.

Place each of the different vegetables in their own bowl. They MUST be marinated separately so that they retain their own vibrant colour and don't bleed into one another. Whisk together the vinegar, water and salt and pour over the vegetables, little by little, just covering them. If you want to get cheffy, put a little baking parchment over the vegetables to keep them submerged. Marinate the vegetables in the fridge for an hour or so, or perhaps overnight to make them a little more pliable and 'ravioli' like.

continued on page 18...

Whipped Goats' Cheese
300g goats' cheese (be it cheap
  and cheerful or posh and artisanal)
about 30ml milk

Sweet and Sour Dressing
50g dried cranberries or sultanas,
  finely chopped
50g dried golden raisins or apricots,
  finely chopped
50g tiny capers, whole, or large ones
  finely chopped
50g shallots, finely chopped
10g chopped parsley
House Dressing (see page 172)

Assembly
alfalfa sprouts
hazelnuts
edible flowers

WHIPPED GOATS' CHEESE / I like to peel furry goats' cheese and perhaps keep the peelings for a boiled up goats' cheese cream for a pasta or similar. Chop the cheese and whizz it in a food processor with a little milk until it becomes velvety and smooth. Place it in a bowl, or even better (and more professional), in a piping bag for easier application.

SWEET AND SOUR DRESSING / Combine all the ingredients in a bowl and loosen with a little house dressing (or use your favourite dressing recipe) – beautifully colourful, sweet, sour and salty.

ASSEMBLY / Drain the coloured vegetable slices carefully and place on some kitchen towel. Put one slice of each coloured vegetable on each plate and pipe a little whipped goats' cheese on top. Top with another slice of the same vegetable. Drizzle a little of the sweet and sour dressing around the mounds of 'ravioli', sprinkle with alfalfa sprouts, grate a little hazelnut over the top, and finish with a few edible flowers.

Chicory Salad

When I worked in Chicago, I learned quite a lot about vegetarian cookery, and I am glad of my exposure to it because it taught me not to be frightened of vegetarians. If you get creative with their food, you will win a fan for life. As well as the vegetarians, there was the odd vegan too, who had an equally good time because of the creative, free-rolling attitude of the chefs. I then discovered a new level, the next level after the vegans: the raw foodists.

Uncooked vegan food might sound like hell, but it is apparently very healthy because none of the goodness is destroyed by fierce heat and 'revolting' meat. When faced with my first 'raw food' request, I started looking at nuts, raisins and cocoa powder in a whole new light; more specifically what you can do with nuts and nut purées – rich, creamy, but also helpfully vegan, and amazingly raw, too.

Brilliantly vibrant pistachio, virgin white macadamia, earthy walnut and sweet almond all made it on to the menu in different dishes, both savoury and sweet.

Soaking the nuts overnight, whether raw or roasted, plumps them and allows them to be blended into a silky smooth and delicate purée, to which you can add sugar or honey for sweetness, or salt and vinegar for a more savoury appeal.

This could be seen as some kind of bastardised Waldorf salad with most of the ingredients missing, but I would stick with calling it delicious – and it just happens to be raw.

Serves 4

Hazelnut Purée
100g hazelnuts
360ml water
60ml vegetable oil
lemon juice or sherry vinegar, to taste
salt and freshly ground black pepper

Assembly
1 head of red and 1 head of white
    chicory, broken into single leaves
House Dressing (see page 172)
½ bunch of Muscat grapes, cut in half,
    or dark black grapes if you can't
    find Muscat
handful of chopped hazelnuts
100g blue cheese (optional, but try
    and use your favourite – I like Stilton,
    Roquefort, Gorgonzola)

HAZELNUT PURÉE / Soak the nuts overnight in the water at room temperature. Or if you want to cheat and un-raw your dish, or are just lazy and have failed to prepare the day before, you can boil the nuts in the water (chop them a bit first) for 10 minutes to set them on their way.

Drain the nuts, reserving the water. Place the nuts in a blender and add 200ml of the reserved water. With the blender running, add the oil and some salt, pepper, lemon juice or vinegar to taste. You may need a little extra water to loosen the purée. Pass through a fine sieve into a bowl.

ASSEMBLY / Spread a layer of the hazelnut purée over the base of a serving dish. Dress the chicory leaves in a little dressing, then scatter them over the purée base. Add the halved grapes and a sprinkle of chopped nuts. If you're feeling in the mood, a few nuggets of blue cheese are always welcome on this dish.

Tomato and Samphire Salad with Peach and Basil

Tomatoes go with many things; I love the classic marriage of tomato and basil, perhaps with some slithers of red onion, mini capers and other fresh herbs, all carefully seasoned and with a great dressing – but it is also fun to introduce new partners.

Try adding a fruity element, such as cherries and raspberries, to the tomato, to emphasise the sweetness; perhaps even stone fruit like peaches, apricots and nectarines, too.

And how about some funky leaves? Rocket we all know, but what about some fire from nasturtiums, the punch of spicy watercress or American land cress, or a salty succulent such as the great British summer treat of samphire. This is another recipe for you to chop and change.

Serves 6

Basil Seed Dressing
10g dried basil seeds (also called Tukmaria, you can buy these in health food shops, Indian shops or a humble garden centre)
100ml House Dressing (see page 172)
a few sprigs of basil, bashed (or use the stalks from the Greek basil below)
salt

Assembly
300g heirloom tomatoes in different colours, cut into wedges, or you could just go for some tasty red ones
100g (about 2) whole peaches, any variety, cut into wedges
50g raw samphire
House Dressing (see page 172)
pickled shallot rings (see Pickles for a Picnic, page 34)
tiny Greek basil leaves (you can pick these up in posh supermarkets)

BASIL SEED DRESSING / Soak the dried basil seeds in the house dressing with the bashed basil and a sprinkle of salt. Leave to bloom for 30 minutes or so until the black seeds turn into little 'frogspawn'. Amazing, and because of the bashed basil, they taste of basil too!

ASSEMBLY / Mix the tomatoes with the peach wedges and samphire in a serving bowl and douse in the well-mixed dressing. Top with some pickled shallot rings, drizzle with the basil seed dressing and garnish with the tiny Greek basil leaves.

Potato, Egg and Cress Salad

We get lots of amazing potatoes from Northumberland, from Lucy Carroll and her fields of heritage potatoes – long ones, short ones, fat ones, knobbly ones, smooth ones, white ones, and all sorts of multi-coloured ones; even some with sensible names.

Boiled potatoes, married with egg, cress and salad cream is a familiar and beautiful-looking dish. Normally banished to the tubs on supermarket shelves with the coleslaw and hummus, here it is given new life.

What better way to refine the Great British potato salad than to funk it up with wonderfully distinct and varied potatoes, delicious eggs, and even a tasty dressing.

Serves 4

Salad Cream
50ml white wine vinegar
1 teaspoon English mustard
15g honey
75ml double cream
salt and freshly ground black pepper

Potatoes and Eggs
2kg new potatoes – if you can find some
    funkier ones, all the better: purple,
    blue, red-skinned, knobbly, etc.
1 bay leaf
a few sprigs of thyme
1 garlic clove, peeled and cut in half
4 eggs, or 12 quail's eggs

Assembly
olive oil
pickled shallot rings (see Pickles for
    a Picnic, page 34)
salad leaves – spicy might be nice here,
    such as nasturtiums or rocket
House Dressing (see page 172)
lemon juice
salad cress

SALAD CREAM / Whizz all the ingredients in a blender and season well with salt and pepper. Set aside in the fridge to thicken up.

POTATOES AND EGGS / Place the potatoes in a pan of salted water (make the water taste like the sea) with the bay leaf, a few thyme sprigs and the halves of garlic, and bring to a simmer (never a rolling boil) for around 30 minutes, until the potatoes are tender. Leave to cool, then peel (if you can be bothered) and slice into thick, double-pound-coin rounds.

Meanwhile, boil the eggs for 6 minutes – or if you're going fancy, boil the quail's eggs for 3 minutes – then refresh under cold water and peel. If you want to do this in advance, keep the peeled eggs in a tub of cold water.

ASSEMBLY / Lay the sliced potatoes flat on a serving plate, dress them with a little olive oil and salt, then swish, drizzle and swirl the salad cream artfully over the potatoes. Cut the eggs in half and lay on top of the potatoes. Touch the top of the eggs with a little olive oil, salt and black pepper, add a few pickled shallot rings and some salad leaves, simply dressed in house dressing or olive oil and lemon juice, and lastly a few sprigs of salad cress.

Bean Salad with Hazelnuts

Serves 4

150g runner beans*
150g fine green or perhaps English
    bobby beans
150g yellow wax beans
150g broad beans
150g cooked peas (or defrosted frozen
    ones would work)
30g chopped shallots
40g chopped hazelnuts
House Dressing (see page 172)
pea shoots and pea blossom (if you can
    track some down)

* in place of the beans used here,
  you could also use borlotti beans,
  flat beans, sugar snaps and even
  mangetout – see what you can find
  and mix it up

Summer does sing berries and fresh fruit, tomatoes and courgette flowers, but to me it also sings peas and beans.

Use whatever you can find for this dish, and try to look closer to home than the Kenyan varieties in the supermarket, which sadly dominate even in the height of summer. There are lots of different beans out there, and us Brits know how to grow them; just check the village shows up and down the country, and meet the old men with their 2-foot-long runners and pebbled-sized broad beans.

This is quite a simple dish of different varieties of beans, dressed with some chopped shallots and lots of crunchy hazelnuts. It goes beautifully with a pork chop, some grilled fish, or as part of any lovely supper for the table. And it is almost as effective with just one type of bean, to be honest. Try and introduce this one to your repertoire.

Cook the beans separately in salted water (make the water taste like the sea) until firm to the bite (not raw and not mushy). You will be able to use the same water for all the beans, but make sure you cook the broad beans last as they turn the water black. If you want to get fancy you could pod all or half of the broad beans, but I don't really mind the skins. Refresh all the beans under lots of cold water and chop the longer ones if you want to.

Mix the beans together with the shallots and hazelnuts, douse in plenty of the dressing, and top with a handful of pea shoots and blossom.

Rainbow Coleslaw

Serves 6

200g thinly sliced or julienned red
    cabbage
200g thinly sliced or julienned white
    cabbage
200g grated or julienned carrots
20g chopped parsley
wholegrain mustard, to taste
House Dressing (see page 172)

Coleslaw doesn't always get the plaudits it occasionally deserves. The soggy acidic stuff found in motorway service stations is a long, long way from this particular version.

Here we have a vibrant, crunchy, healthy, colourful, mayonnaise-free, and I could even stretch to 'fun', coleslaw. Try it; you may never go back to the tubbed stuff again.

Also experiment with shaved fennel, different root vegetables, even parsnips and swedes for a wintry version, with the addition of some tarragon or sorrel through it perhaps. It's very versatile, and another dish to make your own.

Wash the red cabbage in cold water so that it doesn't bleed all over the other vegetables. Mix the cabbages together in a large serving bowl, add the carrots and parsley, and the mustard to taste, and toss with plenty of the dressing.

Fresh and vibrant!

Conductive Food
— commensality and the act of eating together

Meal times should not necessarily be about stuffing our faces (although they can be). They should be about a shared experience.

Meal times should not just be about the food either. Too often we focus only on this element, and although it is clearly an important part, the setting, the company, the lighting, the communication and the comfort all add to the experience, whether at a perched table for two or a large family gathering.

there is a word, not used nearly enough ... commensality.

Meal times, more often than not, bring people together, and there is a word, not used nearly enough in the English language, for the 'act of eating together': commensality, from the Latin *commensalis*.

Another issue that we face in this modern world is around shared food. Food always used to be cooked in batches and shared from a big boiling cauldron, or a hunk of meat from a large joint, but this happens less and less these days. Now we go to restaurants where we order our own portions of plated food, sometimes throwing jealous or even triumphant looks over other people's dishes, wishing we had chosen this or that, sometimes even thanking the good lord that we won the menu roulette that day.

Soup is the most well-known conductive food, easily shared from one big pot, everyone having their hearts and souls warmed together from this one bubbling source. It is a communal experience, and it links us all and brings us closer.

By giving everyone the same food from one source, it is inevitably more of a shared experience, like listening to music together, rather than everyone plugging into different sounds through their headphones.

Commensality is a somewhat lost word in our language, a rather unconsidered part of a meal time, and a concept that many people have forgotten. I would love you to think harder about it. Try and shake off some of the TV dinners, ask younger (and guilty older) ones to put down the phones, and use meal times to connect.

Food can bring us all that bit closer, and meal times can be more than filling a gap, but only if you allow it to happen.

souper conductor soup!

Green Soup

As a nation, we do love a good soup. It is probably something about being frugal and thrifty, perhaps left over from rationing during the war, as much of our infamous food culture is. It's heart-warming, and pretty easy to make: boil and blend, and only a couple of steps in between.

We chop and change our soups in the restaurant every week, but always serve a 'cup o' it' for a light lunch with our Soda Bread (see page 176).

Soups can be very underwhelming, bland and watery or overly-thick. Concentrate on the final consistency and some very careful seasoning. I suggest adding butter at the end to enrich the dish, and a squeeze of lemon juice or vinegar to bring it alive and counter the richness. But not too much.

Serves 6

50g butter, plus 100g extra for
   blending (optional)
250g potatoes, chopped into small
   pieces
250g onions, finely chopped
2 garlic cloves, crushed
1 litre water
200g greens – baby spinach, parsley,
   wild garlic, nettles, lovage (only
   use 50g as this is very strong) or
   watercress – use one of them, or
   a mixture, anything green and delicate
splash of double cream (optional)
grated zest and juice of 1 lemon
   (optional)
salt and freshly ground black pepper

Melt the butter in a large pan and cook the potatoes, onions and garlic for about 5 minutes until soft. Add the water, season well, and cook out for 15 minutes, then remove from the heat and add the greens.

Whizz the soup in a blender; for a little richness you could add a splash of cream or the extra butter at this stage. Check for seasoning and maybe add a little lemon zest and juice to make it sing, but only at the very last minute as it will not be helpful in keeping your green soup green.

Serve with croutons, or a poached egg, or even a slice of cheese on toast.

  Modern British Food

Onion and Cheddar Soup

There is something really lovely and unseasonal about this soup – nothing is locally sourced, foraged or home-grown. This seems to go against all current food trends in this country, but it does hold its own against any dish.

This can be cobbled together with very little, and it was created during one of those real-life moments of writing a menu without any money in the bank and nothing in the fridge. We came out strong with this one, though. It will warm your soul, fill your pockets and make you friends. Just add hot crusty buttered bread rolls.

It is like velvet if you cook the onions out enough, and blended and emulsified with the Cheddar creates one of those truly savoury dishes that the Japanese call umami. This is a warming, connective and conductive dish if ever there was one. Keep it close to your heart.

Serves 6–8 (with leftovers)

500g onions, roughly chopped
200g potatoes, roughly chopped
2 garlic cloves, crushed
bouquet garni with thyme, bay leaves
  and parsley stalks
100g mature or strong Cheddar (none of
  that mild business – get some posh
  stuff if you can manage it), grated
1 teaspoon English mustard powder
a few tablespoons of white wine vinegar
salt and freshly ground black pepper

Put the onion, potato, garlic and bouquet garni in a lidded pot and just cover with water. Season well and put the lid on. Cook over a medium heat for around 30 minutes until soft (the onions have to be very well cooked and translucent). Once cooked, discard the bouquet garni and remove and reserve some of the water (more than you would think) so the soup isn't too thin; you can always add some back in later as you are blending.

Whizz the soup in a blender, adding the grated cheese and mustard, and perhaps some of the reserved stock too if you need to adjust the consistency. Season well with the vinegar, salt and pepper.

Serve with wholegrain mustard croutons or hot crusty buttered bread rolls.

Mushroom 'Tea' and Hot Buttered Crumpets

I practically lived on crumpets as a student, eating them with everything – cheese and pickle, smoked salmon and Philadelphia (posh student alert), scrambled eggs and bacon, and how about devilled kidneys or soft cod's roe… But crumpets will always be associated with teatime, and the more obvious butter, and possibly honey.

As a proud Englishman I also live on tea, so I am bound to be slightly in love with this type of dish. Soups are one thing, fine French consommés another, but a Great British savoury 'tea', be it beef, game or mushroom can be a thing of refined beauty. The marriage of tea and crumpets, brought up a level here, would be a great light lunch or as the start of an interesting multi-course menu. Or you could just make the crumpets on their own.

Everyone loves a bit of crumpet, don't they?

Serves 6

Mushroom 'Tea'
1 onion, sliced
3 garlic cloves, crushed
1 small celeriac, washed, peeled and sliced
vegetable oil
10g chopped thyme
450g button mushrooms, sliced
1.5 litres fresh vegetable or mushroom stock, or use stock cubes
120g dried porcini or ceps
500ml water
60g egg whites (about 3 eggs)
175ml Madeira wine
sherry vinegar
salt

Crumpets
225g strong bread flour
5g salt
10g caster sugar
7g dried yeast
150ml lukewarm water

Assembly
butter, at room temperature
quartered cooked mushrooms (optional)
chopped tarragon (optional)

MUSHROOM 'TEA' / In a wide saucepan, fry the onion, garlic and celeriac in a little vegetable oil for 5 or 6 minutes, until they get a nice bit of colour. Add half the thyme, the button mushrooms and stock, and cook out on a rolling boil for 30 minutes. Strain the stock into a pan and leave to cool, preferably overnight. (You could blend the cooked celeriac, mushrooms and onions into a tasty purée to serve with fish or meat.)

Place the dried mushrooms in a large bowl, cover with the water and leave to rehydrate for 30 minutes or so (or even overnight). Drain the mushrooms, reserving the water for the broth, and chop them finely.

Mix the egg whites, Madeira, the chopped rehydrated mushrooms and the remaining thyme in a bowl. Add to the pan of cold stock with the reserved mushroom soaking liquor and place over a low heat. Whisk the mixture hard at first, then leave it undisturbed. The scummy, frothy egg white will settle at the top of the pan. Once simmering, remove from the heat and leave for 30 minutes to settle before straining it through a muslin or J-cloth into a bowl or clean pan. You should be left with a clear amber liquid with a good mushroomy taste. Season well with salt and sherry vinegar. This freezes very well for future use.

CRUMPETS / Mix all the ingredients together in a bowl and leave in a warm place covered with a clean tea towel for an hour or so to come together and bubble up.

Grease or oil spray some cookie cutter rings (approximately 8cm diameter) and place them in a non-stick frying pan. Give the mixture a gentle stir through and spoon it into the rings until about half full. Cook over a low heat until bubbles start to show, then remove the rings, flip the crumpets over to cook the other sides briefly, and remove from the pan (the crumpets only want to be cooked 90 per cent on their bottoms).

ASSEMBLY / Reheat the crumpets in a toaster and serve with a scoop of the mushroom and tarragon butter. If using, place a few quartered cooked mushrooms in the bottom of 6 teacups, sprinkle with a little chopped tarragon, and serve alongside a teapot filled with the steaming hot mushroom tea. Chin chin!

Modern British Food

Fish Soup

Fish soup, a brilliant dish that seems to have stayed on the menu, is a simple blended soup of leftover fish bones, some tinned bits and dried spice bobs, a glug of booze and some very careful seasoning at the end.

I learned this recipe from the legend Rowley Leigh at the iconic Kensington Place in Notting Hill, a restaurant I used to walk past every day on my way to art college in the 1990s, dreaming of one day being rich enough to eat there. My dream came true five years later.

First I ate there a couple of times, then one day I plucked up the courage to ask for a job. This was four years into my cooking career, and having been rather brainwashed by Michelin stars and faux French cuisine, it was the first place I worked where I was cooking real food for real people; the kind of people who came back week after week, sometimes even a few times a week. Rowley taught me the fine balance between the comforts of everyday food such as a bowl of steaming fish soup and an omelette or steak, and the delicate sprinkles of the finessed seasonal treats such as grouse, fresh anchovies, sea kale and blood oranges.

This is how I write menus for the restaurant today: a few dependable classics with some unknown and surprising delicacies.

This is a keeper of a dish, dangerously (some might say unfashionably) unseasonal, delicious in the right hands, and heart-warming. It will satisfy the soul, and will cost next to nothing.

Classically served with a pot of spicy mayonnaise with a fancy French name with too many 'll's in it (rouille), some grated Gruyère and leftover baguette croutons, we elevate it somewhat – though still ending up with a messy, stringy, cheesy soup-cum-stew – with the addition of a very refined prawnless cracker made with tapioca. We make our own in the restaurant, but you can use shop-bought rice paper that is fried into a pillow to place your jewel-like treats on top of.

Serves 6–8

Fish Soup

1kg fish bones and offcuts/scraps – less
    heads, more carcasses (flat fish works
    well, as does meaty salmon, which
    ours is mostly made of because of the
    large amounts of salmon flesh we get
    through due to our popular Parlour's
    'Back Door' Smoked Salmon, see
    page 43)
100g fennel, roughly chopped
100g carrots, roughly chopped
100g leeks, roughly chopped
100g onions, roughly chopped
1 small tin (200g) tomatoes
1 generous glass of white wine
1 teaspoon each of fennel seeds, star
    anise, black peppercorns, coriander
    seeds
a few sprigs of thyme
2 bay leaves
1 whole garlic head, cut in half
100g rice, cheap and cheerful rather
    than perfumed and refined (it is just
    used to thicken)
Tabasco, to taste
white wine vinegar, to taste
salt and freshly ground black pepper

Rice Crackers

6–8 sheets Vietnamese rice paper
vegetable oil

Assembly

50g finely chopped mature Cheddar
50g finely chopped smoked salmon
    (ideally homemade, see Parlour's
    'Back Door' Smoked Salmon,
    page 43)
10g caviar, if you are feeling flush (or
    lumpfish, between you and me, for
    just a little luxury)
50g soured cream
50g Spiced Mayonnaise (see page 169)
fennel fronds, to garnish

FISH SOUP / Combine all the ingredients except the rice and seasonings in a large bowl and leave to marinate overnight.

In the morning, empty everything into a stock pot, just cover with water and add the rice. Cook over a medium-low heat for 90 minutes, then blend using a large stick blender (or a smoothie maker), bones and all, tasting and seasoning with the salt, pepper, Tabasco and white wine vinegar as you go. If it is too thick, add a little water. Once seasoned well, pass through a fine sieve. The recipe makes quite a lot of soup, but it freezes very well.

RICE CRACKERS / To puff your rice crackers, heat 2cm of oil in a frying pan over a medium heat, and when hot enough (bubbles should form around the end of a wooden spoon), add a sheet of rice paper, with tongs pressing down and moving it. In a few seconds it will puff into a light, flat cloud. Remove and drain on kitchen towel and repeat for each of the remaining crackers.

ASSEMBLY / Dot the crackers (one each) with jewels of Cheddar, smoked salmon, caviar, soured cream and the mayonnaise, garnishing with fennel fronds.

To serve, give each person a warm bowl with a garnished cracker inside, and pour the soup on top.

Duck Liver Pâté

The story goes that my wife didn't actually marry me for my fading good looks, nor my long-winded and occasionally funny story-telling ability – but in fact for my cooking, and more specifically, for this dish.

Not only do I have the same name as my dear wife – Mrs Jessie, as she is now known – we also have a shared love of offal. So for our first date I thought I would play to my strengths and her loves, and cook for her – I made pig's liver faggots. She survived the ordeal and luckily I was granted a second date, and for that I cooked again, but this time chose more of a banker of a dish, my liver pâté. I won her heart, and the rest is history.

This is a dish we always have on the menu: sometimes we scoop it, sometimes we serve a slab of it, sometimes we whisk and pipe it, and sometimes we even serve it inside savoury profiteroles. Now there's a revelation.

Serves 6

½ onion, finely chopped

2 garlic cloves, crushed

1 bay leaf

1 sprig of thyme, roughly chopped

250ml alcohol – 100ml brandy, 50ml sherry (if you are feeling flush), 100ml port (or more of one than another, depending on what you have to hand); also works well with red wine, Marsala, or you could even stretch to whisky

400g duck livers, or chicken or even goose livers, if you can find them

1 teaspoon pink salt or salt petre, if you can find it – it is not critical, but helps the dish stay pink and appetising; often the pâté will oxidise and become rather grey without it – it's all about the look (if you can't find it, leave it out)

3 eggs

400g butter, melted

freshly ground black pepper

Place the onion, garlic, bay, thyme and alcohol in a pan and cook for around 10 minutes, until wet and reduced but not soupy. Leave to cool.

Preheat the oven to 150°C/130°C Fan/Gas Mark 2.

In a blender or food processor, blend the livers with the pink salt or salt petre, the eggs and the cooled reduction, gradually add the melted butter and season well. Pass through a sieve – the mixture should be pale and creamy looking. Check the seasoning, as cold food does seem to dull the taste. It may seem rather weird tasting blended raw livers, but you really have to if you want to have an idea of how the final product is going to taste. I dare you.

Pour into teacups, Kilner jars or into a terrine mould lined with cling film. Place them in a deep roasting tray and fill the tray with boiling water to halfway up the sides of the dishes you are using. Cover the whole thing with foil and CAREFULLY place into the oven so as not to spill or jiggle the mixture too much. Cook for around 20 minutes until there is a faint wobble; it may need another 5–10 minutes, but keep an eye on it. If using just one terrine mould it might need around 40 minutes in total. Remove from the water bath tray and leave to cool, then place in the fridge to set for a good few hours.

This is perfect for sharing with fresh soda bread (see page 176), or even better yesterday's bread, some chutney, funky ketchup (see page 168), or even just some chopped apple jelly left over from making the gala pie (see page 40).

Cook this recipe for a sweetheart and you may just win them over; not guaranteed, but it might just help.

Pickles for a Picnic

Seasoning is something taught carefully to a young chef. But the art of seasoning is a career lesson, never ending, finding the ideal balance of salt and pepper, and countering that with acid and sometimes sweetness, too. As a professional you try and season things highly, more bravely and more confidently than you ever would at home, and with repetitive tasting you start to understand and are more considered as to what a dish might need.

Regardless of all the health scares and anti-salt propaganda, at the most basic level everything needs salt, and as a human being we need and crave it. Salt is certainly the most obvious seasoning. Pepper adds another dimension, whether it's the harsher, spicier black pepper, freshly ground, or perhaps a more subdued white pepper, which lots of professional kitchens seem to be keen on. Then there is acid, which sounds like a dangerous word when associated with food, and in home kitchens is rarely considered.

I have had confused looks thrown at me from new chefs in my professional kitchen, watching me season a vat of 100 litres of fish soup with celery salt (see page 171, ground fennel seeds, table salt, white pepper, Tabasco and, finally … white wine vinegar: 'Chef, what are you doing!?'

When I worked for two-Michelin-starred chef Michael Caines, he taught me to take a small sample of a dish, hold it back to one side, then carry on seasoning the big pot. It is amazing going back to what you thought was delicately seasoned as a comparison to the finished product, which hopefully sings, dances and leaps out at you.

When we talk about making caramel, we often talk about being brave: don't undercook the caramel, let it go dark. When we talk about seasoning, be brave with that too; occasionally you will push it too far and overdo it, but if you risk in this life, you will also be rewarded. As everyone knows, the more you practise, the better your judgement.

We are much more used to acid in our food than you might think, be it in ketchup or brown sauce, chutneys and relishes, a wedge of lemon with fish or squeezed over a salad. Vinegars range from thin and mild rice wine, to deep sweet and sour balsamic, to the more complex sherry vinegars, and all can be used for seasoning. Along with the salt, pepper and acid, you might also need to counter or soften with sugar, even with savoury dishes.

Thai food is a very obviously exciting cuisine. It has colour, heat, sour notes, saltiness, sweetness, spice, and that fifth savoury taste of umami. I believe that people are so attracted to Thai food because of this vibrancy.

Sadly, vibrancy is not a word often used to describe British food: we love pickles with our beige cheese, with some overcooked grey cold meat, or perhaps with a brown plate of fish and chips (pickled egg or onion). I would like to try and change that, to highlight the use of pickles in more dishes, bringing them up and literally tickling your taste buds by giving them the sweet and sour touch.

I would love you to have a play, to see how you can introduce pickles to some of your dishes, be it salads, roasted meats, grilled fish, or even soups. They are a great way of elevating a dish from good to great, adding a crunchy texture, some bright colour and much-needed vibrancy.

Over the obvious pickled onion recipe that I've given you here, on the next page are some other ideas for pickling: all are encouraged and some might even be traditional. Please consider whether the food is cooked (giving a softer texture) or raw (for a bit more crunch), and that the vinegar will affect the colour as well, especially with green vegetables, which will inevitably turn brown.

  Modern British Food

Over the years we have tried any nunber of vegetables, not just limted to the following, some of which can be seen in the image on page 41:

radishes

shallots

celery and fennel

carrots

beans

cucumbers

chillies

red cabbage

cauliflower

fruits, such as diced apple, cherries or grapes

samphire and sea purslane

spring onions, tops and bottoms

mustard seeds

seaweed

We have also done little pickled jellies made with gelatine or agar-agar, pickled ice cubes in cold soups, vinagery gels and sauces. All ideas are welcome – have a try yourself.

Serves 6 (with leftovers)

200ml white wine vinegar (but do experiment with red wine vinegar, malt, sherry, Champagne)

140g caster sugar

1 bay leaf; herbs such as thyme and rosemary, or something fragrant like tarragon or dill; spices such as coriander seeds, cloves or cinnamon (all optional)

200g shallots, carefully sliced into neat rings (also works well with baby onions, sliced red or white onions, but I love the little rings of shallots – they are great in salads and help bring a zing to the dish)

Bring the vinegar, sugar and any herbs or spices to the boil in a pan, then remove from the heat. You could leave everything inside the pan while cooling, but at some point you need to strain the liquor before use (very important). You need to consider what you are pickling: will it take well to cooking it out in the liquor and softening for a few minutes, or should it be poured over hot and then left to cool. For pickled red onions, for example, use red wine vinegar perhaps, and strain it on to the onions HOT – they go fluorescent.

Those vegetables best suited to a hot pickle liquor poured over and just left to cool would be: radishes, shallots rings, cucumbers, chillies, red or white cabbage, cauliflower, fruits such as diced apple, cherries or grapes, samphire and sea purslane, spring onions (tops and bottoms) or fresh or dried seaweed.

Those best suited to a few minutes cooking in the pickle liquor before cooling would be: celery, fennel, carrots, beans, seeds such as pumpkin or mustard seeds (although these are best brought to the boil a few times in fresh water before cooling in this liquor). You could even make some pickle liquor and freeze it in ice cube containers. Then, when you're serving a cold soup such as a white or red gazpacho, cold cucumber or watercress soup, just add a cube or two for a sweet and sour edge – I have stretched it and called it pickled ice.

So, for this recipe, pour the hot pickling liquid on to the raw shallot rings. Leave for a few hours at least before using, and they will almost keep forever.

Chestnut Hummus

Legend has it that someone came into our professional kitchen having had a few too many the night before, and made that quite simple and well-known dish of hummus. Being in rather a fragile state, sadly they forgot most of the vital ingredients, but luckily they did remember those two important components that make a hummus: olive oil and lemon juice. Annoyingly, they forgot the chickpeas and tahini.

Quite what it has to do with its Middle Eastern cousin is rather beyond me to be honest, but this hummus could change your life. It has been a mainstay on the Parlour menu for a few years now, simple, satisfying, and has probably received the most comments of any dish on our whole menu.

Cut with a sherry vinegar caramel infused with rosemary (known as a gastrique), and served with fresh, plump homemade pitta bread, it's sweet, sour, moreish, and rather surprising. The pitta freezes well (but don't feel awkward about buying pitta bread instead), and the caramel stuff (a key part of this dish) will last forever.

Like many dishes in this book, it is accessible and familiar, yet with an element of intrigue and the unknown. I love the comforts of the well-travelled road, but I also love a bit of excitement. Don't you?

Serves 4–6

Rosemary Sherry Caramel
150g caster sugar
50ml sherry vinegar
sprig of rosemary

Hummus
500g vacuum-packed whole chestnuts
250ml water
10g caster sugar
5g salt, plus extra to taste
1 garlic clove, crushed
100ml olive oil
lemon juice, to taste
salt and freshly ground black pepper

Assembly
1 stick celery, finely sliced
pickled red onions (see Pickles for a Picnic, page 34)
picked parsley leaves
chestnuts
Rosemary Pitta (see page 173)

ROSEMARY SHERRY CARAMEL / Make a caramel: place the sugar in a small pan, add a little water – say 50ml – and bring to the boil over a medium heat. When it starts to turn to a light brown, watch it like a hawk, and when it is dark, very dark and almost burnt (be brave), take it off the heat and, to stop it cooking any further, pour in the vinegar. BE VERY CAREFUL – it will spit, bubble and dance, so stand back and be gentle. It will also leave an intoxicating caramel and vinegar pouff – do it near an open window, even outside, and only once you have done it will you know what I am talking about. It will subside when cool, don't worry. Add the rosemary while still warm and leave to infuse overnight at room temperature (it will become thicker in the fridge).

Strain the caramel on the day of using. It should be a good runny honey texture, and the bonus is it keeps forever out of the fridge. It should be sweet and sour with a little rosemary edge (and is also lovely drizzled lightly on your roast lamb).

HUMMUS / In a large pan, boil the chestnuts, water, sugar, salt and garlic over a medium-low heat for around 30 minutes, until the chestnuts are soft and starting to fall apart. Strain through a sieve, reserving the water if there is any left, and blend the chestnuts with the olive oil in the best blender you have, checking for seasoning and adding lemon juice to taste, and possibly a little of the reserved water to reach the consistency of normal hummus. Transfer to a piping bag and set aside in the fridge.

ASSEMBLY / To plate up, pipe a splodge of the hummus on to each plate, cleverly twisted like those in the Middle East do it. Cover it in finely sliced celery for a bit of crunch, a few strands of pickled red onions and some picked parsley leaves. Drizzle with your sherry caramel, grate over a little chestnut in a cloud to finish, and serve alongside the cooked pitta.

Attenborough's Neolithic Eggs

A tongue in cheek history...

David Attenborough, as you know, is a TV personality famous for his wildlife and natural history programming. His almost equally famous brother, Richard, was a film director and occasional actor, well known for his role in *Jurassic Park*. Now as much as David loves the Jurassic period, he is actually more fond of the Neolithic period. Little did you know.

So to celebrate these two Great British personalities, and a pivotal period in our planet's history, I present to you Attenborough's Neolithic Eggs.

In China, and at Easter-time in Greece and in some of the Baltic States, they do this thing with eggs – sometimes called 'tea eggs' – sometimes to celebrate a festival, and sometimes just because. My dear mama has been experimenting for a good few years with natural dyes for her spinning and knitting, and traditional onion skins were a total revelation to me, producing a terracotta colour great for egg shells. But what if I crack the eggs...?

Serves 4

4 onion skins, roughly chopped
1.5 litres water
8 eggs
Aioli (see page 169), to serve (optional)
Celery Salt (see page 171), to serve
(optional)

In a large pan, boil the onion skins in the water for 10 minutes, then remove from the heat. Leave overnight to infuse at room temperature, and the next day bring to the boil again.

Add the eggs to the boiling water for 8 minutes, then take them out and refresh under cold water, or in iced water if you can find some ice. Crack the egg shells lightly all around to give a cracked effect, and when the onion water is completely cold, add the eggs to it and marinate in this naturally dyed water, onion skins and all, making sure the eggs are nestled into the skins and properly submerged. They are good with a 24-hour bath, but even better with a 48-hour bath.

After this time, peel the eggs; the dye will have penetrated the cracks and left the eggs with a mysterious 'Neolithic' effect, looking like a dinosaur egg or something made of marble. Keep them in clean, clear tap water until ready to serve.

Serve with the aioli and celery salt, or build into a funky and prehistoric salad of some kind.

Gala Pie – the Pork Pie with an Egg

Based on the classic French dish of pâté en croûte, with its fancy pastry work, truffled jelly and cleverly constructed terrines of many meats, this is an understated, modest English version of chopped pork and a few herbs, covered in a hot water pastry – and if you hit the jackpot, a magical, never-ending egg yolk through the centre!

Instead of the miscellaneous jelly that you normally find in a pork pie, I have replaced it with a delicious apple juice jelly as a lovely and surprising foil to all that pork, egg and pastry.

The pastry recipe is enough for one large loaf tin. If you're feeling adventurous you could make a few smaller ones, but I prefer to slice a wedge from one long pork pie as I think you get a better meat and pastry ratio this way.

Serves 12

Pork Pie Filling

1kg pork, the fattier the better, preferably pork belly, no skin please – 500g minced and 500g cut into 1cm cubes

85g pistachio nuts – these look great, appearing as flecks of green running through the pie, but you could also use dried fruit such as golden raisins and apricots, or chopped fresh or dried apple or pear

10g salt

a good pinch of ground white pepper

10g black mustard seeds

10g white mustard seeds

30g chopped sage and thyme, perhaps even some rosemary

15 eggs

Pastry

50ml milk

125ml water

100g beef suet

450g plain flour, warmed in a microwave (not hot)

pinch each of salt and freshly ground white pepper

PORK PIE FILLING / In a large bowl, mix all the ingredients except the eggs together. Leave the mixture, covered, in the fridge to come together and to allow the flavours to get to know each other for a few hours.

Cook the eggs in a pan of boiling water for 6 minutes. Refresh under cold running water, peel and set aside.

PASTRY / Line a terrine mould or loaf tin cleverly and carefully: firstly with baking parchment, across the bottom and up each side, hanging over the sides aplenty; don't worry too much about the ends. Then take a 50cm length of foil (or about 20cm longer than the size of your tin) and fold lengthways into a 5cm strip to line the mould lengthways, with plenty hanging over the ends. You are going to have to take the pie out of the mould once it is cooked, and sometimes this is a literal sticking point. Take care of this and you will be fine.

Heat the milk, water and suet in a pan for 5 minutes, stirring until the suet has dissolved; do not allow it to boil. Pour this over the (warm) flour, salt and pepper in a bowl and, using a stand mixer or by hand, combine to form a dough. Knead for a few minutes until glossy and smooth, if a touch greasy.

Set aside a quarter of the mix for the pie top, which must be wrapped well in cling film and kept warm (near the oven, perhaps) while you roll out the rest to the required shape, big enough to fill the bottom and sides of the mould – this should be about the thickness of a pound coin. If you do this while the pastry is still warm, it is much easier to work with. The pastry should line a large terrine mould, with extra left over. Drape the rolled pastry carefully into the mould so as not to disturb the parchment and foil lining, pushing well into the corners and allowing the pastry to flow over each side to be trimmed afterwards.

continued on page 42...

  Modern British Food

ASSEMBLY 1 / Fill the mould with half of the meat mixture, leaving a hollow canal down the middle to cradle the cooked eggs. In order to have the never-ending egg yolk through the middle, the eggs need to be trimmed down by a ridiculous amount. Roll with it. Cut the ends of each egg to the yolk and push them into the pork canal, fitting them in tightly; you will be surprised how many you can actually fit inside. All the egg trimmings and any leftover whole eggs can be used to make a lovely Potato, Egg and Cress Salad (see page 22). It's always better to have too many than too few.

Cover the exposed drainpipe of egg with the rest of the meat, mounding it up into a dome in the middle. You have to be sure to overfill the mould as it will shrink with fat rendering. Egg wash all the exposed pastry around the edges; this will help the top form an impenetrable seal.

Preheat the oven to 180°C/160°C Fan/Gas Mark 4.

Roll out the rest of the pastry for the lid, and place that over the top of everything, firstly pushing it down as flush as you can on top of the meat, then closing around the edges. What you really want is to push the join around the edge of the mould hard, so it ends up being the thickness of one sheet of pastry rather than the thickness of two sheets joined together. Trim the excess pastry from around the edge and crimp it as delicately and fancily as you can. Screw some holes into the top, big enough for you to fit your little finger inside. This lets out steam while cooking and will also be used to pour rendered fat out, and to fill the pie with the jelly when cooked and chilled.

Egg wash the whole thing and place the mould on a tray in case it leaks fat in the oven. Bake for about 45 minutes–1 hour, until the filling is at an internal temperature of 65°C (use a fancy thermometer), or a skewer is warm to the touch when spiked into the middle.

Remove from the oven and leave to cool at room temperature for an hour, then tip upside down very carefully, supporting it well, and let the fat come out of the holes; this will be replaced by the apple jelly when cold. Chill in the mould, ideally overnight, before adding the jelly.

APPLE JELLY / Place the gelatine leaves in a bowl of cold water and leave for a minute or so until soft. Bring 100ml of the juice to the boil in a medium saucepan. Drain and squeeze the gelatine leaves, then add them to the hot juice and stir until melted. Remove from the heat, add the rest of the juice and stir well. Strain into a jug with a nice lip on it. This is more than enough for filling one lovely pork pie and is much better than that mysterious pork jelly you normally get.

ASSEMBLY 2 / When the pie is very cold, take it carefully out of the mould using your paper and foil combo. Check around the pie for any holes or folds that may leak jelly. Wrap the whole thing tightly in cling film, making holes in the top, and fill the cavity with the apple jelly. Chill overnight again to set properly and eat within a few days, with a blob of ketchup and some spinach leaves dressed in olive oil.

Brilliant for a posh picnic!

Assembly 1
1 egg, lightly beaten

Apple Jelly
5 gelatine leaves
500ml apple juice (I prefer the cloudy stuff myself)

Assembly 2
Apple Ketchup (see page 168)
baby spinach leaves
olive oil

Parlour's 'Back Door' Smoked Salmon

It is rumoured that in some Scandinavian countries they actually cook salmon on a plank. They soak cedar wood in water, then steam/bake/roast the salmon on the wet wood, taking flavour from the wood as it heats and cooking the salmon at the same time. Genius! But enough about Scandinavia. We don't do that, we just serve salmon on a plank. And our own salmon at that.

Our smoked salmon is called 'Back Door' smoked salmon because, believe it or not, it is in fact smoked just outside the back door of the kitchen.

We marinate the fillets of salmon whole (using the bones to make the fish soup on page 31) in dark brown sugar and salt for 24 hours, then wash it off and smoke the fish with apple wood in our little backyard smokery.

Some have gone so far as to say it is the best smoked salmon they have ever had, but you be the judge. We cut it thick and serve it with a wedge of lemon, whipped butter and freshly baked soda bread (see page 176).

Cured salmon with lots of chopped dill, known as gravadlax, can be made very easily at home. It is also delicious, keeps well, and is another brilliant fridge basic. You can flavour your cured salmon with fruit (think lemon, lime or other citrus fruits), herbs (tarragon, dill and even mint can work), alcohol (people do it with vodka, Pernod or absinthe), and even vegetables (think beetroot or fennel). Experiment with it, use a combination of a few of these ideas, make this dish your own, make it fun and personal.

Hot smoking uses hot smoke, believe it or not, and a hot-smoked product will have a cooked and flaky finish, whereas cold-smoked salmon, which is what we do, comes out tight, dry and with an almost waxy texture as a result of the marinade. It will come out of the cold smoker the same texture as it goes in.

Smoked salmon is a classic, but if you ever did want to make a cheat's version, you could marinate it in smoked salt (from fancy food shops), which gives a similar smoked finish. Or just buy a cold smoker…

Smoked Salmon

Serves 6

400g salt (this could be substituted for
smoked salt (available online) – if so,
skin the salmon beforehand)
120g soft dark brown sugar, or use
white sugar for a less rich and
complex finish
½ side of salmon, skin on (approximately
600g)

You will need
access to a cold smoker or Bradley
Smoker (see method)

Mix the salt and sugar well – you could even use an electric mixer – and scatter half
on a non-reactive tray large enough to accommodate the salmon fillet snugly. Lay the
salmon fillet on the salt mix, skin side up, then scatter the rest of the salt mix over the
salmon, making sure it is well covered. If putting fillets side by side, please make sure
the two fillets don't touch and that there is marinade between them. Cover with cling
film and leave in the fridge for 24 hours.

The dry marinade will become soupy and wet; this is the extraction of moisture from
the fish by the salt, so don't worry about it. If you are feeling frugal, you can reuse the
marinade for a second time. The salmon should be firm to the touch, a little leathery
even, and noticeably 'cured'. Wash the fillet thoroughly in cold water, then pat dry with
kitchen towel and lay it on the smoking rack.

If you have access to a cold smoker or a Bradley Smoker, make sure it is set up
for cold smoking and follow the individual machine's instructions for setting up and
smoking. Leave the salmon in the smoking chamber, either hanging or skin side
down, for 4 hours, then remove and wrap in cling film and store in the fridge. Though
not essential, all fish smoked in this way is best made a couple of days in advance for
the flavours to settle and mellow, and will keep in the fridge for up to 2 weeks.

Cured Salmon Alternative

Serves 6

150g salt
150g caster or granulated sugar
150g grated raw beetroot (optional, but
adds a dramatic red streak), plus extra
to serve
grated zest of 2 lemons, limes or
oranges, plus extra to serve
½ bunch dill or tarragon, chopped, plus
extra to serve
10g freshly ground white pepper
½ side of salmon, skin on (approximately
600g)

Mix all the ingredients, except the salmon, together in a bowl and lay half of the
mixture in a small, non-reactive tray. Place the fish on top, skin side up, and lay the
rest of the marinade mixture over the fish. Cover with cling film and leave in the fridge.
Cure for 24–36 hours, depending on the thickness of the fillet, until firm to the touch.

Wash the fillet under cold water and pat dry with kitchen towel, then cover tightly with
cling film. This will keep in the fridge for about a week.

When you're ready to serve, scatter a few chopped herbs on top of the fillet, or a
little grated beetroot on the side, with the fresh zest of citrus fruits to show what it is
marinated in. Serve with a soured cream, cucumber and orange salad and hot brown
toast, or soda bread (see page 176) might be even better. It's amazing for a dinner
party – and even better as leftovers for breakfast or brunch.

Stilton Custard with Walnuts

Surely an Englishman's two favourite things: Stilton and custard. Not often found together in a dish, but this was partly inspired by the Swiss ski-party dish of fondue, and another classic, the French summer dish of crudités, or more specifically *le grand aioli*. But more than anything, it was inspired by a certain Parmesan custard with anchovy toasts from chef Rowley Leigh. I just gave it the funky injection it needed. I might even have improved on it. You be the judge.

A cheesy, custardy dip, a savoury crème brûlée if you will, best served with some unusual shaped and coloured crudités – choose some interesting and delicious-looking vegetables – and also leftover bread (we call it yesterday's bread), crisped up into some crunchy croutons, the custard topped with a nutty praline to force the question: 'is it a sweet or a savoury dish?'

On the face of it, it's a fairly weird idea – cheese, sugar, cream, nuts and vegetables – but in essence, think fondue! Think garlicky French olive oil mayonnaise and the endless things you can stick in it. Think of the sharing, of a group of lovely people huddled around this intriguing and colourful spread. It works really well for about 95 per cent of people – they see it as a revelation; and the other 5 per cent ... well, who cares for them? They are almost certainly the strange ones.

Serves 6–8

Cheese Custard

100ml milk
250g Stilton, or your favourite blue cheese (could also work with goats' cheese or Cheddar; some have even made a career out of making it with Parmesan)
100g egg yolks (about 5 yolks)
500ml double cream
salt and freshly ground black pepper

Assembly

Nutty Praline (see page 178), made with 200g walnuts
crudités (kohlrabi, golden cherry tomatoes, lettuce hearts, broccoli, funky heritage carrots, beetroot, radishes…)
crusty bread or croutons

CHEESE CUSTARD / Blitz the milk, cheese and egg yolks in a blender until smooth. Pass through a sieve, then add the cream and season; it shouldn't need much – salty cheese and all that.

Preheat the oven to 150°C/130°C Fan/Gas Mark 2.

Pour the custard into one large dish or several little jars, or even ovenproof teacups might be fun. Place the dish, jars or cups inside a large baking dish and pour in enough boiling water to come halfway up the sides. Cover the whole baking dish loosely with foil and cook for about 40 minutes (depending on the size of the dishes) – it should retain the 'crème brulée wobble'. Remove the dishes from the water to cool. These will keep in the fridge for a good few days.

ASSEMBLY / Serve the custard topped with the praline and with a huge selection of crudités alongside – be as daring or as fun as you like. You can stick numerous weird and wonderful vegetables in this lovely savoury custard, and crusty bread or crostini-type croutons would also be a great addition. The custard is best served at room temperature, but could also be served cold or even slightly warm.

Modern British Food

Pork Scratchings!

Pork scratchings have been a mainstay of pub menus for as long as people have been drinking warm beer in this country. Salty, fatty, cheap-as-chips pork skin that makes people happy, greasy and thirsty – and as a bonus for the landlords they sell even more beer as a result. Everyone wins – except anyone who is waiting for the pay check to come home after work on a Friday night.

Crunchy, porky, delish, and seemingly very simple. Try it, you will be surprised how complicated it actually is.

Trim the pork rind so there is only a little fat attached. Place in a pan, cover well with water and simmer for 2 hours until very tender, topping up with water if you feel you need to. Raw pig skin is very tough, and in the hot water it will eventually break down to be jelly-like.

When you think it is done, take it out of the water GENTLY to keep it in as big pieces as possible, and layer the pieces flat on a tray, with baking parchment in-between. Leave in the fridge for several hours, or preferably overnight, so that it will set flat.

Once chilled, trim off more of the white fat and preheat the oven to 200°C/180°C Fan/ Gas Mark 6. Using very strong scissors (the rind can be a bit tough), cut the rind into strips, then place on a baking tray lined with baking parchment, spreading the strips out well so the pieces don't stick together. Sprinkle with a little too much salt (the fat really needs it) and bake, covered loosely with foil, until golden and crunchy, 25 minutes or so. If you don't cover it, you will have to scrub the oven afterwards, as it really does snap-crackle-and-pop everywhere. I usually give it a blast uncovered for the last 5 minutes to give it an extra puff.

Serves 6

1kg pork rind (not just pork fat)
flaky sea salt
Simple Apple Compote (see page 179),
   to serve

Serve on more paper (we use yesterday's menus to soak up any grease) with a little pot of warm apple compote, sweet and tart.

Long-Lost Quiche

I call this a 'Long-Lost Quiche' because of its loss of popularity with the 'young' these days. Like the pork pie and the pork chop, the chicken Kiev and even the Arctic roll (all dishes that have been much abused and misinterpreted over the years, yet helpfully improved upon and resurrected in this book for you), the quiche should hold strong its position in the hall of fame and 'Great Dishes of the World'. Cook this and remind yourself of how lovely a quiche can really be.

Quiche has sustained its popularity, mainly for its ability to magic whatever you have in the fridge into something sensual, heart-warming and shareable. Here I give a few ideas, but just use this recipe as a guide and add whatever you like or whatever you have to hand. Be generous with the contents, be generous with the seasoning and be generous with the portions, please.

Some people try cooking it in rings, but I have found there to be too much chance for leakages. A pie dish or ceramic quiche dish (even better) will prevent it from leaking, no matter if you have a few holes in your pastry. Bear this in mind, there is nothing worse than a leaky and half-filled quiche for lunch.

Serve with a simple salad, or something funkier from the salads in this book (see pages 16–23).

Serves 6

Quiche Mix
500ml double cream
100g egg yolks (about 5 yolks)
50g egg (about 1 egg)
salt and freshly ground black pepper

Assembly
Savoury Pastry cases (see page 177),
    6 small or 1 large
egg yolk, for sealing

Tomato Tarts
red onion marmalade
sliced spring onions
sundried tomatoes
black pepper

Ham and Mushroom Tarts
slow-cooked onion
diced ham
sautéed mushrooms
chopped parsley

Leek and Cheddar Tarts
stewed onions
cooked leeks
diced Cheddar
chopped thyme
black pepper

QUICHE MIX / Blend, mix or whisk all the ingredients together in a bowl and season bravely.

ASSEMBLY / You can fill your quiche with absolutely anything. Here I've given you some classic ideas for you, but please feel free to run wild.

Preheat the oven to 180°C/160°C Fan/Gas Mark 4.

Seal your cooked pastry case(s) with a lick of egg yolk to make sure they don't spring a leak. Add a generous quantity of your chosen filling ingredients. Pour over the quiche mix and try to have a few of the pretty tomatoes, leeks or tangles of spinach (depending on your filling) sitting high up out of the veil of savoury custard for a bit of visual impact.

Bake in the oven for about 20 minutes for small cases or 45 minutes for one large case, until there is still a slight wobble, but always check for any uncooked custard in the middle. When you're confident it is cooked, remove from the oven and let it rest for at least an hour before trying to slice.

Serve with a simple green salad and let the quiche do the talking.

Quornish Pasty

The village of Quorn is actually in Leicestershire, far, far away from the Cornish coast. In the 1980s someone devised a recipe for a 'plant-based meat alternative', and we have been trying to get our heads around it ever since.

A funny rift on a Cornish classic, without the need to kill any animals. Some might be hard pushed to tell the difference. This is deeply savoury, meaty and satisfyingly filling, despite the lack of meat.

Serves 6–7

Pastry

450g strong white flour (plain will still
   do the job, though)
20g baking powder
1 teaspoon salt
120g butter, cold and diced
2 eggs
100ml water

The Quornish Mix

50ml olive oil
150g swede, chopped into 1cm cubes
150g celeriac, chopped into 1cm cubes
200g mushrooms, quartered – button,
   chestnut, or wild if feeling flush
2 garlic cloves, peeled and chopped
3g chopped thyme leaves
1 bay leaf
200g Quorn mince (available at most
   supermarkets)
30g plain flour
100ml red wine
200ml water
grated zest of 1 lemon, to taste
balsamic vinegar, to taste
Celery Salt (see page 171) and freshly
   ground black pepper

Assembly

1 egg, lightly beaten
sea salt
chopped thyme (optional)

PASTRY / Mix the flour, baking powder and salt together in a bowl, add the diced butter and rub through by hand or use an electric mixer. Add the eggs and water and bring together into a smooth dough. Roll into a ball, wrap in cling film and rest in the fridge for around 30 minutes, if you can.

THE QUORNISH MIX / Heat the olive oil in a large pan and cook the swede and celeriac for about 5 minutes, then add the mushrooms with the garlic, thyme and bay leaf and cook for another 5 minutes. Add the Quorn, followed by the flour, stirring in well, then add the red wine and water. Season with celery salt and pepper, and add the lemon zest and balsamic vinegar to taste.

Cook out for 15 minutes, until it's the texture of a classic Bolognese sauce. Remove from the heat and leave to cool.

ASSEMBLY / Preheat the oven to 180°C/160°C Fan/Gas Mark 4.

Divide the pastry into 100g pieces and roll each one out to a round of about 18cm in diameter. Add around 80–90g of the Quornish mix to one side of each circle, brush the edges with egg and fold over to seal. Try and do the neat tuck-and-fold that's the Cornish pasty tradition.

Brush the outside with more egg, then sprinkle with sea salt and perhaps some chopped thyme. Bake in the oven for about 25 minutes, or until golden. They are great eaten hot, or even quite nice cold.

Kitchari – Kedgeree

The brilliant Simon Hopkinson, once a ground-breaking masterchef and now having to 'make do' with just being a rather good magazine contributor and book author, is famously the writer of *Roast Chicken and Other Stories* (apparently THE 'Best Cook Book Ever Written'), and more recently he wrote a book called *The Vegetarian Option*. Indeed, the vegetarian option is always quite a sticking point for a lot of restaurants. There is only so much wild mushroom risotto that one man can take, and to have an interesting, innovative and original dish such as this makes you stand out, and gives you some street cred with those not wanting to eat flesh.

That sometimes-famous posh breakfast or 'High Tea' dish of kedgeree is rumoured to have come from the more complex and exotic dish from India, 'kitchari'.

This one is a little closer to the original in that it is not about the colonial British additions of smoked haddock and lots of chopped parsley, but a vegetarian dish of rice, lentils and a few spices, and I've added my two pence worth with an egg and some buttermilk sauce.

You can make it into a sloppy/fluffy and familiar risotto/biryani-style kedgeree dish, either as the recipe below or with the addition of some chicken or smoked salmon, or the more traditional smoked haddock.

Serves 6

Kitchari Mix

4 tablespoons vegetable oil
1 teaspoon nigella seeds (onion seeds
   to you and me)
1 teaspoon mustard seeds
½ teaspoon turmeric powder
½ teaspoon cayenne pepper
½ teaspoon ground ginger
½ teaspoon curry powder
2 garlic cloves, chopped
150g shallots or onions, roughly
   chopped
150g basmati rice, rinsed
100g red/yellow/split peas or lentils
   of some kind, rinsed
½ teaspoon Celery Salt (see page 171)
500ml water
grated zest and juice of 2 lemons
salt

Fried Onion Bhajis

1 onion, cut into rings
100ml buttermilk
20g curry powder
½ teaspoon ground ginger
1 teaspoon turmeric powder
40g self-raising flour
½ teaspoon salt
vegetable oil

Minted 'Yoghurt' Dressing

100ml buttermilk, or natural yoghurt if
   you can't find any buttermilk
grated zest and juice of 1 lemon
1 teaspoon chopped mint
salt and freshly ground black pepper

Assembly

7 eggs – 4 whole, 3 beaten
70g plain flour, seasoned with salt
   and pepper
150g breadcrumbs (panko are best)
vegetable oil, for deep-frying
baby spinach leaves
olive oil
lemon juice
nigella seeds

KITCHARI MIX / Heat the vegetable oil in a large pan and toast the spices for 2–3 minutes. Add the garlic and shallots, and cook for another 5 minutes, then add the rice and lentils, season well with the celery salt, and a touch of normal salt if needed, cover with the water and cook out for 20 minutes or so, until the water has evaporated and the rice and lentils are cooked – top up the water if necessary to ensure the lentils and rice are cooked. Add the lemon zest and juice for freshness – the rice and lentils should be fragrant, well seasoned and slightly acidic from the lemon. Use immediately or set aside to cool if preparing in advance.

FRIED ONION BHAJIS / Soak the sliced onions in the buttermilk for at least 5 minutes, or even overnight, if necessary.

Toast the spices for a couple of minutes in a dry frying pan if you can be bothered (it is better but not essential), then combine with the flour and salt in a bowl.

Drain the onion rings, then toss them in the seasoned flour until well coated.

Heat the vegetable oil in a deep-fat fryer set to 180°C and fry the onion rings for 2–3 minutes, or shallow fry in plenty of oil for a minute or so, until golden and crispy.

MINTED 'YOGHURT' DRESSING / Combine all the ingredients together in a bowl and season well.

ASSEMBLY / Boil the 4 whole eggs in a pan of water for 6 minutes. Drain, cool under cold running water and peel.

Preheat the oven to 200°C/180°C Fan/Gas Mark 6.

Place the seasoned flour, beaten eggs and breadcrumbs in separate shallow bowls. Roll the peeled eggs in the flour, then in the egg wash, and then in the breadcrumbs. Heat the oil in a deep-fat fryer set to 180°C and fry the eggs for a minute or so until golden, then transfer to a baking tray in the oven for 12–14 minutes until cooked through.

To serve, warm up the cooked kitchari, in a pan or even in a microwave, top with some of the freshly fried onion bhajis (reheat if necessary), baby spinach leaves dressed in olive oil and lemon juice, a pool of the minted 'yoghurt' dressing and a sprinkle of nigella seeds.

Comforting, familiar and excitingly exotic.

NOTE / You could add 200g of mixed smoked and unsmoked fish to the kitchari during the last 10 minutes of cooking the rice to give it another dimension.

Scrambled Eggs

You mum's scrambled eggs might be a little like your mum's pork chops (see page 80): nostalgic, comforting, familiar, but perhaps you might have had better elsewhere.

This is a rather decadent recipe, with way too much of a particular ingredient, but it could actually change the way you make eggs. If you see scrambled eggs as a healthy and light lunch, maybe stick to the boiled or poached versions, as these won't allow any other secret, delicious, dangerous ingredients to be used...

Serves 1

100g eggs (about 2 eggs)
70ml double cream
salt and freshly ground white pepper
Soda Bread (see page 176), to serve
    (optional)
Parlour's 'Back Door' Smoked (or
    Cured) Salmon (see page 43), to serve
    (optional)

Place the eggs and cream in a non-stick pan and cook slowly on the hob over a low heat, stirring constantly for a couple of minutes, until the eggs are softly set. Season to taste.

I recommend serving the eggs with fresh soda bread, and they go particularly well with our smoked or cured salmon, too.

Trout with Peppers and Almonds

The Spanish have this wonderful romesco sauce of almonds, peppers and bread, which goes great with chicken, boiled eggs, potatoes and, luckily, fish. I have stolen the sauce and run away with it to create perhaps not the most traditionally British recipe in this book, but a fine one, and it sings of summer to me, wherever you are.

Serves 4

Romesco Sauce

250g roasted red peppers (use jarred
    or roast them yourself)
3 garlic cloves, peeled and chopped
50g toasted almonds
75g white bread (use gluten-free if you
    must!), crusts and all
20ml sherry vinegar
75ml olive oil
salt and freshly ground black pepper

Trout and Peppers

4 x 120g+ trout portions – whole small
    trout or fillets (you could also use
    salmon, or Arctic char is getting
    popular), skin on
vegetable oil
4 roasted peppers (red and yellow),
    skin rubbed off and stalk and seeds
    removed, roughly chopped
500g cooked new potatoes, cut in half
1 small fennel bulb, cut directly across
    into 1cm-thick rounds, then steamed
    or boiled until tender
sherry vinegar

Assembly

a handful of toasted flaked almonds

ROMESCO SAUCE / Blitz the peppers, garlic, almonds, bread and vinegar in a food processor with a little seasoning, and slowly drizzle in the olive oil. Transfer the sauce to a bowl and re-season. It will never be the smoothest sauce, especially with the crunchy nuts in it, but boy is it good. The sauce will keep well in the fridge for a few days, and it is great served warm or cold with any number of things.

TROUT AND PEPPERS / Cooking the fish over a barbecue or grill would be amazing for this dish, but if you haven't got access to this rather un-British set up, here is an indoor cooking option for you.

Season the fish portions well on both sides with a bit more salt and pepper than you think might be right, and place gingerly into a hot pan, skin side down, with a little vegetable oil. Be careful not to overcrowd the pan; do it in batches if it's looking too snug. Cook them over a high heat until the skin is coloured (you might need the extraction fan on high for this as it will cause a bit of smoke), and then turn over and keep cooking for another 3 minutes or so, until just cooked through.

Remove from the pan on to a plate and leave them by the oven to rest for 3–4 minutes. Add the roasted peppers, new potatoes and fennel to the pan and turn down the heat for the time it takes to rest the fish, basting and turning to warm and flavour the ingredients in all the fishy oil. Remove from the pan and sprinkle with a little sherry vinegar for a kick.

ASSEMBLY / Spread a good tablespoon of the sauce over each plate, place the fish in the centre and sprinkle the cooked peppers, potatoes and fennel over and around. Sprinkle with the toasted almonds for a final crunch.

Sea Bass with Lots of Lovely Green Things

Oliver Peyton, the 'authority', as he is now, on Great British food, famous for his judging role on the *Great British Menu*, and my ex-boss from the glory days of The National Dining Rooms at the National Gallery in Trafalgar Square, reminded me that you not only have to cook for yourself when designing a restaurant menu, but to always remember to cater for everyone on the table, and all tastes and preferences. As much as I might like Cow Pie (see page 95), there has to be an option on the menu to satisfy the more delicate friend, or stereotypically, the delicate lady friend. And that might not always be you.

As an opinionated business owner with vision and drive, I set up the restaurant and therefore the food and drink on offer (and décor) to suit my own tastes, but I must really consider others.

Some people love going to restaurants, and some even love food too, but it is not everyone's cup of tea. Lots of people eat out through duty and social responsibility, some don't even like food that much, and the balance of dishes on a menu must reflect that. So no matter how whacky and delicious some things may be, always try and offer a safe option for those less adventurous and excitable than you.

Girls, as we all know, love sea bass. Girls love green things and luckily they also love lots of lovely anythings – so the bets are they are going to love this dish. Vague and mysterious-sounding, the name gives an idea of the dish rather than being outright clear as to what it really entails. Feel your way through the recipe and make it your own.

I have suggested a green sauce to go with this dish to tie the fish and the vegetables together. Culinary glue some may call it; keeping the dish together. This sauce is a bit more famous in other places though, in Spain it is *mojo verde*, in Italy they might called it *salsa verde*, while we keep it simple with the literal translation of exactly what it says on the tin – green sauce. It is a great accompaniment to fish, chicken and even fried halloumi, or steamed leeks. Keep this close to you and use it again and again.

You can chop it up and make it rough and rustic – like all good things, this unfortunately require a few knife skills and some of your precious time. Or, you can also put everything in a blender and purée the lot in 30 seconds. Over to you and your priorities.

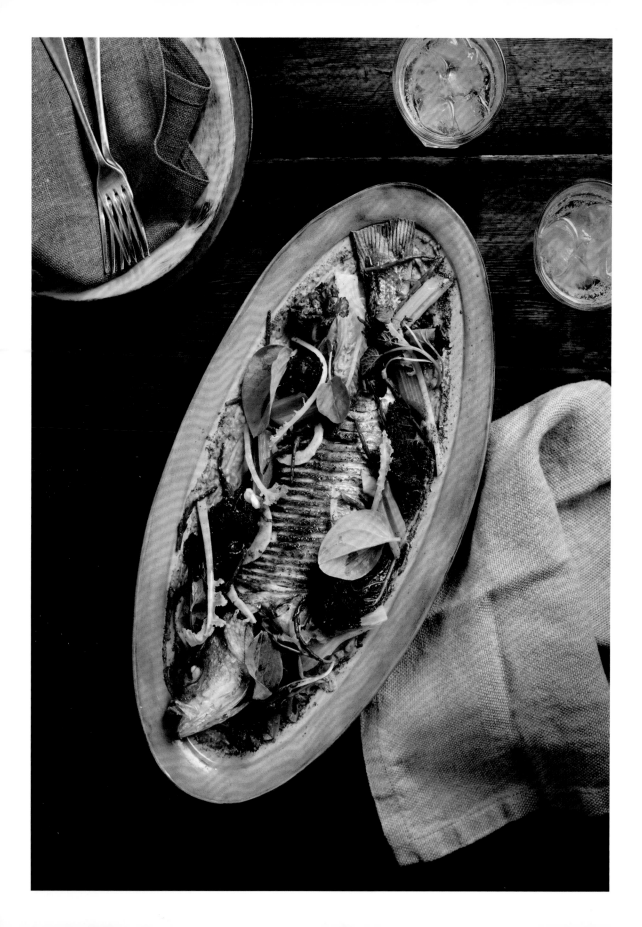

Serves 6

Green Sauce

200g parsley

75ml olive oil

50ml vegetable or sunflower oil

25ml red wine vinegar

½ red onion, finely chopped

75g capers, chopped

grated zest of 1 lemon

salt and freshly ground black pepper

Sea Bass and Greens

200g green vegetables per person,
   from a selection of whatever you
   might find on your travels – as well as
   the peas, asparagus, leeks, broccoli
   and beans you would probably think
   of, be a little more adventurous and try
   some of these:
runner/wax/bobby beans
cabbage, cavolo nero or other less
   exotic species
kohlrabi
fennel
samphire
spinach
chard
broad beans
spring onions
cucumber
gem lettuce
bok choy
(raw options): sliced apple and
   avocado for some texture and
   contrasting acidity; even the
   samphire, gem lettuce or shaved
   fennel could be added raw
olive oil
grated zest of 2 lemons, plus a squeeze
   or two of juice
6 whole (gutted and scaled) sea bass,
   or sea bass fillets (you could also
   use salmon, trout, grey mullet or
   seabream)
knob of butter (optional)

Assembly

lemon wedges, to serve

GREEN SAUCE/ Blanch the parsley in boiling and very salty water for a minute or so, then plunge into iced water, or at least very cold water. Squeeze dry, then whizz in a blender with the olive oil, vegetable or sunflower oil and vinegar. Transfer to a bowl, add the red onions, capers and lemon zest, then mix and season well.

SEA BASS AND GREENS / Preheat the oven to 180°C/160°C Fan/Gas Mark 4.

Cook your selection of vegetables to your liking – boiled or steamed. They will each require slightly different timings, so try and cook them separately if you can. Place all the cooked vegetables in a bowl and, while hot, dress with olive oil, lemon zest and a touch of lemon juice, and salt.

Place the whole fish on a baking tray and roast in the oven for 15–25 minutes, depending on the size of your fish, until a skewer comes out easily from the cooked flesh. If using fillets, fry them in a pan, in a good glug of olive oil and a knob of butter: about 6 minutes on the skin side and a couple of minutes on the flesh side, or under a hot grill for 10 minutes, skin side up.

ASSEMBLY / Put a swirl of green sauce on each plate, add the fish and a tangle of the beautiful green vegetables on top. Always try and serve fish with a wedge of lemon on the side – acidity, remember!

Halibut with Citrus Fruits and Olive Oil Mash

This book is all about flavour marriages and contrasting textures. Soft with crunchy, acidic with rich and soothing, raw with cooked. Here we have a lovely bit of steamed fish with some silken olive oil mashed potatoes and citrus fruits to cut through the richness.

Serves 6

Olive Oil Mash

500g potatoes, peeled and chopped – Maris Pipers and King Edwards work well

100ml hot milk

100g butter, melted, plus an extra 50g for reheating

75ml olive oil (extra virgin, if you are feeling flush)

salt and freshly ground black pepper

Halibut

6 x 120g+ halibut portions (you could also use brill, turbot, plaice, cod or even salmon), skin removed

Assembly

500g spinach leaves

grated zest and segments of 1 orange, 1 lime, 1 pink grapefruit and 1 white grapefruit; and the juice from the carcass of the fruits

olive oil

lime wedges, to serve

rock salt, to serve

OLIVE OIL MASH / Boil the potatoes in pan of salted water, and when cooked but NOT falling apart, strain them and leave them in the empty pan to steam through. It is always a great idea to let them steam to get rid of excess water. Mash them as you would normally, incorporating the hot milk and melted butter, and season well. If you want to get really fancy you could pass it through a fine meshed sieve to help achieve that cheffy, glossy finish.

This mash can be made a few hours in advance and then reheated, to help with the stress of putting all this together. When reheating, add the extra butter and the olive oil to enrich it; if it looks oily, whisk it and it should come together.

HALIBUT / Season the fish on both sides. In a steamer, or over a pan of simmering water (with some lengthways-cut carrots acting as a trivet), steam the fish gently for 3–4 minutes, covered with a lid, until opaque.

ASSEMBLY / Pan-fry the spinach briefly, adding salt and pepper, until starting to wilt down, then strain through a sieve.

Chop the fruit segments and add to the juice and zest with a little seasoning.

Place a tangle of spinach on each plate, then put your fish carefully to one side and scoop some olive oil mash on the other side. Drizzle a little of the chopped citrus fruit vinaigrette over the fish and spinach, and pour a little olive oil over the mashed potatoes. Serve with a wedge of lime if you like, and a sprinkle of rock salt for a salty kick.

Mackerel with Gooseberries

Oily fish such as mackerel, sardines and salmon (use whatever you can find from those choices) work well with the acidity and sweetness of fruit. If you have a blowtorch at hand, and are using fillets of fish rather than whole fish, use it for maximum impact, even do it in front of your dining companions – it is theatrical and slightly dangerous, but oh, what fun!

Serves 4

4 good-sized mackerel fillets, or a whole fish (you could also use sardines or salmon fillets)
olive oil
table salt
shaved (or very finely sliced) fennel
House Dressing (see page 172)
Gooseberry Compote (see page 179)
crusty bread, to serve
lemon wedges, to serve

You will need
a blowtorch

Preheat the oven to 180°C/160°C Fan/Gas Mark 4.

Oil the fish fillets well all over and salt the non-skin side. Place the fillets on a metal tray, skin side up, with space between them to breathe, as it were. Perhaps place another upturned tray underneath the cooking tray as some sort of protection (the top tray will get very hot – be careful not to burn the bench or table you are working on). Blowtorch the skin side, searing the skin of the fish until blackened and burnished, then salt the skin. The fish might need a couple of minutes (or 4) in the oven if a little undercooked all the way through.

If using whole fish, as shown here, score the skin of the fish for beautiful presentation, put a non-stick tray, dress with olive oil, salt and pepper and bake in the oven for about 10 minutes.

Dress the fish fillets with a salad of shaved fennel dressed in house dressing, and serve with some chunky gooseberry compote, crusty bread and a wedge of lemon. That is all you need.

Great British Sunday Lunch
—with or without roasted meat

Mother England! I have travelled and lived abroad, and there are many things that I love and miss about my beautiful country while I am away. As well as a full English breakfast, I love Pimm's, black cabs, fish and chips, Wimbledon, the Proms – but the real clincher is the traditional Sunday lunch, more often than not at a local pub, with lots of gravy, and always finishing with a crumble ... a crumble served with ice cream, whipped cream AND custard (see pages 180, 181 and 109).

The English do know how to roast meat, and also know of some great accompaniments, especially on a Sunday. The Yorkshireman who invented the pudding from a leftover Frenchman's crêpe batter was a true genius.

> ## The Yorkshireman who invented the pudding from a leftover Frenchman's crêpe batter was a true genius!

And whoever thought of serving up a bit of fire and spice with the meat, too – fire in the form of that wild British weed, horseradish, and spice from our fierce English mustard – what a brilliant idea.

The choice of meat for your Sunday roast is a tricky one though, I think beef often wins more often than not – but only when other people are cooking it. There's certainly a skill to the perfect rosy pink roast beef. A little bit too undercooked and there is always that embarrassing grimace of pretending you're enjoying it, when actually 'it looks like it is still moving Douglas?!', and all your English friends are being really kind about it ('Oh, I do love rare beef, don't you Anthony... Do pass the horseradish' and 'No, no seconds for me thanks, delicious though...'), whilst thinking one thing ('THIS IS BLOODY RAW!'). Then again there is always that horrible discovery of going too far the other way, and OVERCOOKING the damn thing.

Cat Stevens was the first to declare 'The first cut is the deepest' and he was so right. Slicing into dangerously undercooked, or even worse, disappointingly overcooked roast beef is such a family trauma. The expectation levels are sky high for a home-cooked roast; but the amount of juggling involved and managing to get together potatoes, vegetables, Aunt Bessie's, Bisto, Coleman's and even have time to get the plates ('heat the plates please Trevor, I do hate a cold plate...') and cutlery together, all in time, often gets the better of people, and at least one element, if not most of them, goes wrong.

The beef might always look great and then there is the agonising reveal with the first cut. Hero or villain? Saviour and miracle worker, or are you just about to be written out of the family will with the grey slabs of bone-dry chewing gum topside piled on the plate. 'Pass the gravy Tracy! You might even need to get more on by the looks of this one dear!'

Chicken though, is probably the popular choice when it comes to home roasts; something about it not being as critical when you leave it in for an hour too long. The usual story was often along the lines of 'mother was good at the weekly Sunday roast but MY the chicken needed that gravy, it was dryer than the Serengeti...'

Pork and lamb, or more exotic alternatives like kid goat or venison, will always play second fiddle, although slow cooking a shoulder of pork and a leg of lamb until it falls apart have taken much of the tension out of a family get together at the weekend. And indeed, nut roast probably deserves a section of its very own, so we have done exactly that.

> I am not about to give you a lesson in meat cookery, but instead help you achieve the best accompaniments to win the hearts of your Sunday guests.

The salt crust pastry I've given in this chapter is an impressive way of cooking meat and fish: think leg of lamb, whole chicken, loin of pork or rump of veal; whole sea bass, trout, or even a salmon if your oven is big enough; it also works for lovely things like kohlrabi, potatoes or butternut squash. Experiment and make a spectacle of your Sunday lunch sometime. But please remind yourself how much salt goes into this dish and how horrible it must be to eat – the pastry is merely a vehicle for the cooking rather than a lovely addition to your Sunday lunch. The ingredients on page 70 should make 1kg total, which can be rolled out large enough to cover a large fish, a leg of lamb or a whole chicken.

However, sadly I am not about to give you a lesson in meat cookery, but instead help you achieve the best accompaniments to win the hearts of your Sunday guests.

As good as you might be at roasting meat, you may need a little extra help with the bits on the side; the bits that help you turn a blind eye to the slightly overcooked chicken or the undercooked lamb.

By giving the meal a strong foundation, you are capable of winning many hearts. Think of it: a Sunday roast with a brilliant carrot! Professional-looking Yorkies! A salt-baked chicken! Even homemade horseradish!

Yorkshire Pudding

Traditionally these are eaten only with roast beef, but what is to stop you eating it with roast pork, chicken or lamb – controversial I know.

I have a few top tips: you need a really hot oven and stinkingly hot moulds, and try and remember to cook them through, if undercooked they will deflate once cool. Also, contrary to popular belief, Yorkshire puddings can be precooked a few hours before and reheated before serving. (It all helps with time management.)

This recipe also doubles up as an awesome crêpe batter for Shrove Tuesday, or any other day you might want to test your flipping skills, just add a good splash of milk.

Serves 6

200g beaten eggs (about 4 eggs)
200ml milk
160g plain flour
6 tablespoons vegetable oil

Preheat the oven to 220°C/200°C Fan/ Gas Mark 7.

While you get the mixture ready, place a 6-hole muffin tray in the oven to get it stinkingly hot. Whisk together the eggs, milk and flour in a bowl, either by hand or using a stick blender. Pass the mixture through a sieve.

Carefully take out the hot muffin tray, put a tablespoon of oil in each well, and fill each hole two-thirds full of batter. Cook for about 10–15 minutes, until well risen and cooked through. Serve immediately.

Horseradish

Coleman's jarred is fine, but if you want to really push the boat out, the first challenge is to find a fresh horseradish stick (one of the more difficult requests in this book I fear) and then you have make the stuff. Making it is pretty easy, just be careful when blending, it gets rather intoxicating at stages.

TOP TIP – save a large chunk of the horseradish stick for grating over your finished roast once plated up for the final flourishing touch (see the picture on pages 66–67, middle bottom left).

Serves 6

30g fresh horseradish root, chopped
150g soured cream
10g English mustard
scant ½ teaspoon xanthan gum (ideal, but not essential)
salt and freshly ground black pepper

Blend the horseradish with the soured cream in a food processor, add the English mustard and season well. If you have some, add the xanthan gum to help thicken the sauce, as it does get a little sloppy otherwise. This is best made the day before you want to use it, to allow the flavours to infuse.

Bread Sauce

Best served with chicken, but great with pork and any other 'white meat' you might find. This is a very underrated condiment and not usually in the forefront of people's minds when roasting a chicken. I urge you to revisit this, a real link to the past.

This is not a trendy or a sexy recipe, but they have been eating it as a chicken accompaniment since Henry VIII, and I for one understand why it has been going so strong ever since.

Serves 6

300ml milk
sprig of thyme
1 onion
1 bay leaf
3 cloves
a few parsley stalks
grating of nutmeg
100g white sliced bread, blended
   in your food processor, crusts 'n'
   all; alternatively, use a little less
   (50–75g) of the shop-bought dried
   breadcrumbs – go gently, little by little
70g butter
salt and freshly ground black pepper

Place all the ingredients, except the breadcrumbs and butter, in a pan and bring to the boil. Take off the heat and leave to infuse for 5 minutes, then strain through a sieve on to the breadcrumbs in a bowl. Mix well, return to the pan and reheat, stirring continuously. Add the butter and salt and pepper to taste. Keep warm. If you make it in advance and it starts to thicken up, just add a little more milk.

Carrot Cooking Liquor

This is a great and delicious way of precooking your carrots. Try it, you might well be surprised. They can be served whole, but also cut, either before cooking or afterwards. This should be the best carrot you have ever cooked, and that might even stretch to the best one you have ever eaten!

Serves 6

600ml water
50g butter
10g salt
10g caster sugar
a few sprigs of thyme and tarragon
1 bay leaf
4 large whole carrots or 5 sliced
   or chopped

Add all the ingredients except the carrots to a pan, bring to the boil, then strain on to your whole or cut carrots and gently simmer them in the cooking liquor for the desired amount of time. The liquor can easily be made ahead of time.

Sunday Stuffing

Serves 6

2 garlic cloves, peeled and chopped

1 onion, chopped

60g celery, chopped

1 teaspoon chopped sage

vegetable oil

250g frozen, tinned or vacuum-packed
peeled chestnuts, chopped

125g chicken livers, fried to cook
through and roughly chopped

200g minced chicken, or pork mince
would work too

30g chopped prunes

60g dried breadcrumbs (fresh will
also do)

2 teaspoons chopped parsley

1 egg

salt and freshly ground black pepper

It's great to have some old-fashioned stuffing with your Sunday roast, or any day of the week for that matter. Make it chickeny, make it porky, cook it inside your chicken or on the side – it's a great addition however it comes, and is nearly a dish on its own. This could be made in a larger batch and then frozen in logs or loaves for future Sundays, and added in balls to the roast potatoes for the last 15 minutes if cooking separately. The chestnuts could be replaced with mushrooms, prunes replaced with other dried fruit and the chicken with turkey or duck to go with the meat you might be serving.

Fry the garlic, onion, celery and sage in a pan in a little vegetable oil, season well, and cook for about 5 minutes until soft but without colour, if you can manage it. Add the chestnuts and remove from the heat. Leave to cool.

Preheat the oven to 180°C/160°C Fan/Gas Mark 4. Once the mixture is cool, transfer to a large bowl and combine with the meat, prunes, breadcrumbs, parsley and egg. Season well.

Place little mounds in the holes of a greased muffin tray, or neat piles on a baking tray, or use a loaf tin if you like, and cook for about 20 minutes (or around 30 minutes for the loaf tin, depending on size), until golden. This could also be stuffed into the neck or body cavity of your turkey or chicken before cooking as you would normally.

Salt Crust Pastry

Don't wrap your chosen meat/fish/vegetable in the pastry in advance – they will dry out and become salty. Wrap them and cook them straight away!

Preheat the oven to 180°C/160°C Fan/Gas Mark 4. Mix the flour and salt in a bowl, then gradually add the egg whites and water, and incorporate until you have a nice dough. Roll out the dough with a rolling pin until about 5mm thick, and if not using immediately, leave it in the fridge (well covered please) until you need it.

Wrap your chosen fish, meat or vegetable in the pastry, place it on a parchment-lined tray, perhaps egg washing the outside, and sprinkle with rock salt and chopped herbs to give it a nice finish.

Serves 6

500g plain flour

300g salt

140g egg whites (about 5 eggs)

150ml water

2 eggs, lightly beaten (optional)

rock salt

chopped herbs – think thyme and
rosemary

Cook until golden, fragrant and toasty outside and 'cleverly judged' to be perfectly cooked within. The cooking of your fish, meat or vegetable might take a bit of trickery. To see if it is actually cooked inside, use a metal skewer, which will easily pierce cooked fish or vegetables (undercooked will offer resistance). For meat, you could touch the skewer to your lip as a guide (lukewarm is rare, warm is medium rare, and hot is well done), or read up on meat temperatures and use a precise thermometer for accurate judgment.

Carve at the table for full effect!

Nut Roast with Red Wine Sauce

Nut roast has been a bit of a dirty phrase in the English language ever since it was invented; a dry, hopeless vegetarian offering for those not wanting to kill animals for their Sunday lunch. My rather whacky old spinster great-aunt used to bring her own nut roast to the family Christmas dinner, the first time most of us had ever heard of a vegetarian: 'I just hate the thought of harming something with a face...'

The enthusiasm of those making or ordering the dish is never quite matched by the enthusiasm of those actually eating it. It's never as enjoyable as it promises to be.

This recipe, on the other hand, is moist, tasty, surprising, and even the most blood-thirsty meat eaters might be happy settling down to this with their Yorkshire puddings and roasted carrots.

It is also a brilliantly versatile recipe, with the opportunity to use any of your favourite vegetables – try beetroot for something earthy and colourful, parsnips for something sweeter, or peas and cabbage greens for something more vibrant and healthy – along with your chosen cheese and nuts. But whatever you do, try and sneak some mushrooms in there for added texture – it certainly helps.

Serves 6–8

Nut Roast
2 garlic cloves, chopped
vegetable oil
400g mixed vegetables, chopped or grated or a bit of both – think onions, mushrooms (a must for texture), beetroot, fennel, courgette or squash
200g cooked spelt, white or brown rice, barley, or any other grain you have – even couscous or quinoa would work
100g breadcrumbs – dried are best, but fresh would still work
100g toasted nuts, flaked, whole or chopped (I like hazelnuts and almonds)
100g grated Cheddar or your favourite hard cheese
handful of chopped fresh herbs – think thyme, tarragon, parsley, sage or oregano
grated zest of 2 lemons
2 eggs
salt and freshly ground black pepper

Red Wine Sauce
1 x 750ml bottle of red wine
40g caster sugar
100g shallots, sliced
100g button mushrooms, sliced
sprig of thyme
bay leaf
15g cornflour, mixed into a slurry with a little water (around 3–4 teaspoons)

NUT ROAST / Preheat the oven to 170°C/150°C Fan/Gas Mark 3.

Fry the garlic in a large pan in plenty of vegetable oil for about 3 minutes, until toasty and coloured; if using onions then add them to the pan with the garlic. Next, add the remaining vegetables and cook all together until soft, 10 minutes or so. Remove from the heat and add the cooked grain, breadcrumbs, nuts, cheese, herbs, lemon zest and eggs. Mix together and season well. Test the mix by baking a little patty in the oven and re-season if necessary.

Butter and flour the moulds of a muffin tray, or a traditional 900g loaf tin, then mound the mixture inside. Place a tray under the tins in case of any overspill, and bake for around 20 minutes for the smaller muffins, or around 30–40 minutes for a whole loaf, until a skewer inserted into the centre comes out clean.

RED WINE SAUCE / Place all the ingredients except the cornflour in a pan over a high heat and reduce until halved in volume. Strain the sauce through a sieve or colander, then return the hot liquid to a pan, add the cornflour slurry to thicken, cook out for 5 minutes and season it up with salt and pepper. The sauce will keep in the fridge for a few days, and freezes well too.

ASSEMBLY / Serve the nut roast with all the other Sunday accompaniments (see pages 68–69) and the red wine sauce or your own choice of vegetarian powdered gravy.

Steak and Chops for Dinner

To be a proper man, by definition, you have to be good on the barbecue, take control of situations, drive either a fast or a sensible car, be strong, drink red wine with your dinner, Scotch after your dinner, and eat steak for your dinner (being rather carefree about the vegetable accompaniment).

Sexist assumptions in a restaurant setting are pretty much an everyday occurrence. Thankfully, gone are the days of two menus, one with prices for the man and the other, non-priced, for the lady companion. But we are still faced with dilemmas: who gets the wine list, who ordered the pint of beer, who gets the Cow Pie, who gets the bill at the end? It will still always gravitate towards the man – even today, it will.

Chops are not the most obvious of ladylike foods, but everyone loves a lamb chop, pork chop and Tomahawk beef chop. I dare you to quibble with that.

Chops are a Great British classic, so let's keep the tradition alive, giving it a shot in the arm with a couple of my favourite recipes.

Chops are a Great British classic, so let's keep the tradition alive.

Butters!

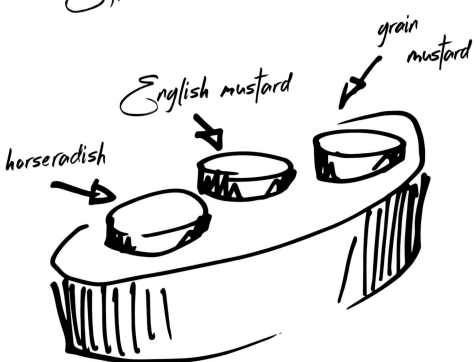

horseradish

English mustard

grain mustard

Veal Chops with Creamed, Sweet and Popped Corn

I love popped corn. I love sweetcorn. I even love Italian polenta and American grits (essentially the same things, yet the Italian dish can't help but sound more fancy than its Yankee relative. I'm also rather surprised we don't have an English version of 'creamed corn', as it grows so well over here). And all of these on one plate with a fat meaty chop is a wonderfully decadent idea. But using popped corn in a dish? Well, it makes sense with all the other elements, I suppose, and it is fun, relevant and adds a certain texture. The spinach is a guilty addition, just to make sure you're eating your greens like your mother said you should.

Serves 6

Veal Chops
6 x 160g French-trimmed veal cutlets
   (you can also use pork, beef or lamb)
200g butter
bunch of thyme, chopped
small handful of sage leaves, chopped
salt and freshly ground black pepper

Polenta
900ml chicken or veal stock
115g quick-cook polenta

Popped Corn
olive oil
50g popping corn kernals

Creamed Corn
1 sweetcorn 'ear', trimmed of any
   greenery, and kernels shaved off
   lengthways with a knife
knob of butter
2 tablespoons water
1 teaspoon caster sugar
100g baby spinach leaves

Assembly
lemon wedges, to serve (optional)

VEAL CHOPS / Smother the veal cutlets in 50g of butter, some chopped thyme and sage, and salt and pepper, and cook under a medium grill for about 4 minutes on each side. Leave to rest for a good 5–10 minutes somewhere warm.

POLENTA / Heat the stock in a pan and season well. Whisk in the quick-cook polenta and cook out for 5 minutes or so, until thick and creamy. Add as much butter as you dare (100g or so), and season well with salt and pepper.

POPPED CORN / To make popcorn, you'll need a heavy-based large pan with a lid. Heat the pan with a little oil, then add some corn kernels, less than half a layer in the bottom, they need lots of room as the kernels expand in volume considerably when they burst and need room to fully 'pop'.

Cover the pan (very important) and heat. The kernels will swell and start to 'pop', bursting out of their skins, so shake the pan regularly to keep the unpopped corn moving. Once the popping sound dies out, remove the pan from the heat and carefully remove the lid. Season with some olive oil or melted butter and a good sprinkle of salt.

CREAMED CORN / In a separate pan, cook the raw sweetcorn kernels with another knob of butter, the water and sugar, and season with salt and pepper. Once cooked through, add the baby spinach and warm until the leaves are wilting.

ASSEMBLY / Spread some of the polenta on each plate, place a veal chop on top, scatter over the spinach and sweetcorn kernels, baste everything with the leftover juices and herbs from the cooked meat, and lastly add the warm popped corn. You could serve this with a wedge of lemon to finish.

Steak with Sm-ash

Sm-ash – the instant mash that is the guilty secret of many an ill-judged parent. So easy to make that even teenagers who have recently flown the nest can give it a go, alongside their overcooked steak, perhaps. And we all have the one dippy friend who was told you just needed to add it to boiled water, so added a packet to the kettle…

I have only ever tried making sm-ash once, to try and work out what all the fuss was about. I made it with a little milk and lots of butter, and it really wasn't that bad. However, sm-ash in this context is a beautifully silky real mashed potato, with the addition of smoke … smoked mash = sm-ash!

Smoke and grilling has also stayed popular, even with the invention of boil in the bag sous-vide cookery and electric kitchens, and everyone loves the flavour of meat cooked over wood and coals; the smoky edge and campfire nostalgia of cooking over a real fire. It might be difficult to achieve those same flavours at home, but you can certainly harness some of it. Think of this as a wonderful mashed potato, rich and decadent, with the addition of a wisp of smoke. And hopefully real smoke at that.

This sm-ash goes really well with beef steak, but also a pepper-crusted venison haunch, or lamb chops for that matter, or even a whole or chunk of fish on the bone. Be brave and experiment.

Steaks will never go out of fashion luckily, and people have been eating roasted meat on and off the bone for thousands of years. These days though, in a restaurant environment, there is more and more pre-portioned and off the bone cookery. All very well, and all very helpful, but try cooking bigger steaks to share instead of thin-cut single portions, this way you get real char, real pinknesss, flavour and moisture, and cooking on the bone adds another dimension, too.

You can buy some mega huge slabs of beef on the bone, and although it might take a bit longer to cook, and might seem expensive, you will be rewarded with a far superior product.

If you want to try different steaks aside from your fillet or rib eye, try something with a little more bite and a little more flavour, perhaps a thick-cut rump, a bavette or an onglet, or even a flat iron steak; see if the butcher can help you try something new.

  Modern British Food

Serves 6

Mash to Smoke

500g potatoes, peeled and chopped –
  Bintje, Maris Pipers and King Edwards
  work well
100ml hot milk
100g butter, melted, plus an extra 100g
  for reheating
liquid smoke (optional)
salt and freshly ground black pepper

Steak

6 whole unpeeled onions (red, white,
  even large shallots)
6 steaks – I love a good bavette for
  flavour and bite, but also love a rib eye
  or sirloin for a little more finesse; never
  been that excited by fillet myself
vegetable oil
2 or 3 garlic cloves, peeled and halved
a few sprigs of thyme
knob of butter
splash sherry vinegar

Assembly

3 Gem lettuces, halved and dressed well
  with House Dressing (see page 172)
English mustard

You will need

access to a cold smoker or Bradley
  Smoker (optional)

MASH TO SMOKE / Boil the potatoes in a pan of salted water, and when cooked but NOT falling apart, strain them and leave them in the empty pan to steam through. It is always a great idea to let them steam to get rid of any excess water. Mash them as you would normally, incorporating the hot milk and melted butter, and season well. If you want to get really fancy you could pass it through a fine meshed sieve to help achieve that cheffy, glossy finish.

At this stage you could add a few drops of liquid smoke (easily available, but not quite the same) or go the full power option and hook up your smoker and smoke the finished mash (see page 43 for smoking instructions). Before smoking, transfer the mash to a shallow, wide non-reactive tray to allow maximum coverage of the smoke.

When reheating, add the extra butter to enrich the sm-ash.

STEAK / Preheat the oven to 200°C/180°C Fan/Gas Mark 6. Place the onions on a baking tray and roast for 30 minutes. Leave to cool, then peel, halve and set aside.

This is a GUIDE to steak cookery rather than gospel, as I have no idea how thick-cut your steaks are or how you might like them cooked. I like my steaks cut thick and cooked bloody – if this is your route, follow the instructions below. Otherwise, the thinner they are, the less time they will need; or the more well done you want them, the longer they will need in the pan.

Season the steaks well on both sides with a bit more salt and pepper than you think might be right, and place gingerly into a stinkingly hot pan with a little vegetable oil. Be careful not to overcrowd the pan; cook them in batches if a little too snug. Cook the steaks over a high heat until well caramelised on one side, about 5 minutes; you might need the extraction fan on high for this as it will cause a bit of smoke (sadly not enough to smoke the mash over). Turn the steaks over, add some halved garlic cloves, thyme and a knob of butter, and keep cooking for another 3 minutes or so, basting the steaks in some of the beautiful herby and caramelised juices they are wallowing in. If you are looking for a steak more on the well-done side, you might want to pop it in an oven preheated to 200°C/180°C Fan/Gas Mark 6 for 5, 10, perhaps even 15 minutes, depending on how well done you really like it.

When you are happy they're done, place them on a plate and leave them by the stove to rest for 5 or 6 minutes. Add the cooked roasted onions to the pan and turn down the heat for the time it takes to rest the meat, basting and turning to warm and flavour the onions in all that slightly burnt fat. Remove from the pan and sprinkle with a little sherry vinegar for a kick.

ASSEMBLY / Place some warmed and enriched smoked mash on each plate with a half of roasted onion, a dressed half of Gem lettuce, a dollop of mustard and a steak cut in half to expose a flash of rosy skill. Be sure to pour any steak juice from the resting plate over the finished steaks.

Steak with Too Many Butters

Steak and butter. A lovely idea. And made all the easier with some pre-prepared butter pulled straight from the freezer. Be it off the barbecue or out of the griddle pan, this is a simple dinner elevated because of a little organisation and foresight.

Compound butter is a great freezer staple. I love to have a few options at hand, and this is a wonderful recipe in which to preserve any leftover flavoursome treats in a butter for a rainy day. Add them to a slab of fish, chicken or steak, over mushrooms or even into a risotto.

Additions well suited for butters, encouraged, and possibly even traditional:

anchovies

cooked (or raw) mushrooms

herbs

truffles

mustards

seaweed

capers, roasted peppers and sundried tomatoes

roasted vegetables

spices, either ground or just crushed in a mortar and
pestle

bacon (use smoked, if you can)

citrus fruit zest and juice

toasted nuts

You could also use a combination of some of the above for specific foods: herbs with mustard or mushroom for a steak; seaweed and capers for scallops; bacon and onions stirred into a plain risotto; or hazelnut and lemon for a whole baked fish, for example.

Serves 4

Compound Butter

120g butter, softened
120g flavouring from the list above (or go
    wild and try something off piste)
salt and freshly ground black pepper

Steak

4 steaks – I love a good bavette for
    flavour and bite, but also love a rib eye
    or sirloin for a little more finesse; never
    been that excited by fillet myself

Assembly

simple green salad
oven chips
Malbec

COMPOUND BUTTER / Use an equal quantity of flavouring (which must be cold before mixing with the butter) to softened butter. You make up the size of the recipe – the weights given here are just a guide.

Beat the butter with a wooden spoon (or you could use an electric mixer with a paddle or whisk attachment), fold in your chosen flavouring and season it really well. Either spread into ice cube trays or pipe on to a tray and freeze; the frozen piped butter can be transferred to a Tupperware container in the freezer.

STEAK / Cook the steaks according to the instructions on page 77.

ASSEMBLY / Serve the steak with some sliced butter on top – you can use one flavour, or a couple if you have been busy; if you want to flash a blowtorch over them to give them a melting helping hand, all the better. Be sure to pour any steak juice from the resting plate over the finished steaks.

Serve with the salad, oven chips and a glass of Malbec.

A 'Remarkable' Pork Chop

For me, pork chops of old are those leathery-shoe-sole chops of childhood. And if we weren't scared off by the tough, anaemic cookery of dear old mother, then the government's insistence on overcooking the bloody stuff to ensure it killed off the parasites of questionable farming practices really was enough to put anyone off for life.

In this country, pork chops don't command the respect and high regard that they deserve, and it is a shame, because they can be a thing of delicious elegance and beauty. Eating a juicy, free-range-organic-off-pink pork chop may be a challenge to those stuck in their ways, but those willing to roll with it will exorcise the demons of mother's grey flip flop and never look back.

Brined for flavour, preservation and to help retain some of those porky juices, it was a revelation to me, and hopefully will be a culinary turning point for you, too. Some might ask why it is 'remarkable', and you can wait until they have finished eating it to answer them; they may well agree with you without needing any further information.

Serves 6

1 litre water
2 bay leaves
2 cloves
½ stick of cinnamon
25g fennel seeds
1 garlic clove, smashed
2 pieces of orange peel (from 1 orange)
75g caster sugar
75g salt
6 x 300g pork chops – thick cut would
  be great, bone in or out, it's up to you
  (meat on the bone is always preferable
  at my table)
Tomato and Samphire Salad with Peach
  and Basil (see page 21) or buttered
  cabbage (optional)
cracked black pepper, to taste

In a large pan, bring half the water to the boil with the herbs, spices, garlic and orange peel. Add the sugar and salt, then remove from the heat and pour in the remaining water cold – this helps cool it down that much quicker. Leave to cool completely – if you can chill this overnight, all the better – then strain before using.

In a non-reactive dish, lay out the pork chops in a single layer, cover with the brine and leave for 2–3 hours in the fridge – the thicker they are, the longer they need to be in the brine. You don't have to use all the brine – just make sure they're submerged; perhaps cover them with a snug baking parchment lid to make sure.

When ready, remove the chops from the brine and pat them dry. The brine can be frozen for use another day.

Grill, barbecue or pan fry the chops until pink (if that's your preference), about 6 minutes each side, depending on the thickness (NOT well done, thank you), and leave to rest. There's no need to add salt as they will be seasoned enough from their brine bath – they might enjoy a little fresh cracked black pepper, though.

When ready to serve, reheat the cooked and rested meat in a pan, oven or under the grill for a couple of minutes to give it a hot edge. Serve with a simple tomato salad (or the slightly more elaborate version on page 21) or even buttered cabbage.

How would you describe the pork chop – 'remarkable'?

Golden Breadcrumbed Everything

A clever trick I have found to create 'deep-fried' foods without a fryer...

My earliest memory of pubs is probably eating scampi and chips with half-a-lime-and-soda, age eight, on a rickety bench outside our village local (The Norman Knight). I did not grow up in an inspired foodie family, and neither was I inspired by food locally. I didn't know what scampi was (bits of fishy something?), but to be honest, the person frying them probably didn't know either. And I had never seen a fresh lime before. This was in the mid-1980s in middle England.

Great Britain was going through its own soul-searching foodwise back then, and with scampi, chicken nuggets, Scotch eggs, fish fingers, onion rings, potato croquettes (the list really could go on), breaded and fried foods have always had a special place in our hearts. Straight from the freezer into the fryer, they have served the service stations, schools, pubs and cafés, even those places a little more high and mighty, very well over the years. There is something easy and consistent about these foods for the chef, something safe, familiar and consistent for the recipient too, and I am one of those guilty of loving them.

Breaded foods need a strong, clear identity inside – they need to be punchy and striking, to contrast with the protective bland golden shell, and there really needs to be an exciting, colourful and upliftingly zingy dip on the side too; think of a fruity condiment like ketchup, HP sauce, apple sauce, even tartare sauce, more often than not with acidity and sweetness. Textural crunchy shells with soft and forgiving centres, dipped or doused in some kind of exotic sauce. A wonderful combination.

A clever trick I have found to create 'deep-fried' foods without a fryer is to dip the finished breaded thing in sunflower or vegetable oil, then place it on a baking tray and straight into a hot oven. It is not quite the same, but it works a treat most of the time. No one will ever know, and there are no pots of dangerous boiling-hot oil to contend with either. Try it, you might surprise yourself.

Chicken Kyiv, Hash Browns and Rainbow Coleslaw

The quintessential pre-prepared British supermarket chicken dish – apparently first stocked in the UK by M&S in the 1970s – it is a happy throwback to a bygone era. It has a history of uncertain beginnings, apparently nothing to do with Kiev in the Ukraine at all, and occasionally nothing to do with real chicken either; its heritage seems to have more to do with garlic and tourism. But that doesn't stop it being a very popular dish, sadly not featured enough on restaurant menus these days.

Luckily, this version also has the authenticity of real chicken and real butter, and the presentation has been given an update. The accompaniments of coleslaw (everyone's favourite partner for fried chicken) and hash browns (inspired by the McDonald's breakfast) are easily found in the deli/freezer aisles of the supermarket, just down the way from the ubiquitous Kiev, if you don't want to make them yourselves.

This is a dish unquestionably inspired by my upbringing and the weekly routine. One of the strange things about the beginnings of this dish is that I hadn't ever actually had a Kiev before I made one for the menu. Luckily I understood the idea, and I knew what I was looking for.

The dish fitted perfectly into my first pub menu; it was in some way British, it transcended class and budget and it was certainly familiar to most – don't most people secretly cook them at home in front of Eastenders? (Sadly I didn't grow up in a family like that… No package meals and certainly no telly…)

Having had the new best-selling dish of the Chicken Kiev on the menu for a year or so, I was then invited to Kyiv by a wealthy young Ukrainian former student of my wife's. We were met by a yellow Porche at the airport and were given a whirlwind tour of the sushi bars, cocktail lounges and penthouse apartments around town. What I really wanted though was a native taste of the traditional Kiev. It's harder to find that it sounds. We were taken to the tourist spots downtown and tried various versions of their 'National Dish'; probably using Chinese garlic and Vietnamese chicken, it came out of the freezer into the fryer for the baying masses looking for that elusive classic dish.

Having eaten six Kievs in Kyiv, and realising mine really was the best one out of all of them, I decided to dedicate my (secret British national dish) Kiev to Kyiv the city and call it a … Chicken Kyiv, and ever since people have been asking why the dish is misspelt on the menu.

This recipe comes in several parts, and is, be warned, fairly complicated. However, it does freeze very well, and the garlic butter can be frozen separately too, so you can spread the load of all the preparation.

I have a very clever top tip…

When deep frying at home, you can always put the old chip pan on the back burner, until smoking and dangerously hot. You might even have upgraded to an Argos multifunctional Value Pro-Stainless Steel home fryer. However, I, and I think there may be others reading this book, have never had a chip pan, nor a fancy deep-fat fryer, but I have a solution to your problem!

Pour some plain oil (groundnut, vegetable, rapeseed or sunflower) into a suitable high-sided container to fit your breaded item. Dip your breaded item into the cold oil and make sure the crumbs are saturated, drain off the worst, then transfer to a parchment or foiled-lined tray and bake in a hot oven (200°C/180°C Fan/Gas Mark 6) until toasty and cooked as per the recipe. All the scary deep-frying avoided, but all the benefits of a golden bread-crumbed something or other.

  Modern British Food

Serves 4

Kyiv

6 whole garlic heads
200g butter, softened
60g parsley, chopped
4 skinless chicken breasts – ideally
    organic; at the very least free-range
    (none of this battery business please –
    that would be so 1990s)
salt and freshly ground black pepper

Panne

70g(ish) plain flour, seasoned with salt
    and pepper
2 eggs, beaten
150g breadcrumbs (Japanese panko are
    best for an even finish)

Assembly

Rainbow Coleslaw (see page 23)
4 Hash Browns (see page 171)

KYIV / Preheat the oven to 180°C/160°C Fan/Gas Mark 4. Roast the garlic whole on a baking tray in the oven for 30 minutes or so, until soft inside. Leave to cool, then cut the tops off and squeeze out the garlicky goodness on to a board. Chop finely into a near purée, then add to the softened butter and parsley in a bowl and mix well until smooth (1). Season it well – the Kyiv gets little other seasoning, so the butter should be beautifully salty. Place in a tub and chill for 30 minutes, then ball out portions (about 70g or so) with a warm ice-cream scoop or garlicky hands (2). (The size of the butter balls determine the size of your Kyivs.) For best results, freeze the garlic butter at this stage.

Top and tail the chicken breasts, removing the fillet from underneath (3), until you are left with a square chunk, about 7.5 x 7.5cm. The trimmings can be used to make chicken nuggets or the beginnings of a curry.

Stretch out a double layer of cling film, put the trimmed chicken on one side and fold over the cling film so it is well covered. With a rolling pin, smash the breast into a flat and fairly even round shape (4). It needs to be approximately 12.5cm round, big enough to wrap around the ball of garlic butter. Peel back one side of the cling film and place the butter in the centre of the flattened chicken (5). Close the chicken around it by bringing the cling film together and twisting it, making a round, stuffed garlic chicken breast ball (6). Repeat with the remaining chicken and butter balls.

To be considered a Kyiv, the chicken needs to be breaded: for this to be done easily, pop the balls into the freezer for a few hours (you could leave them overnight, or even for weeks).

PANNE / Place the flour, eggs and breadcrumbs in separate shallow bowls. Once the Kyivs are frozen, unwrap them from the cling film and roll in the seasoned flour, then in the egg wash and then roll in the breadcrumbs (7). Repeat the egg wash and breadcrumb rolling for a second time – this makes for a better seal and is known as a 'double panne' (8). The breaded chicken can then be left to defrost in the fridge for a few hours, or even for a day or so, and it will be ready for cooking. It's best not to cook from frozen.

ASSEMBLY / Preheat the oven to 200°C/180°C Fan/Gas Mark 6. Heat the oil in a deep-fat fryer set to 180°C and fry the Kyivs for a minute or so, until golden, then transfer to the oven for 15 minutes. The butter should be melted inside, ready to burst and dribble down your chin. Serve immediately on a bed of rainbow coleslaw and a hash brown (9). (See page 2 for an image of the finished dish.)

7

8

9

Fried Brie with Cranberry Sauce

I always use pretty cheap brie for this. You can use an organic-unpasteurised-prize-winning-artisan cheese – just don't tell the cheesemaker what you are using it for, as you might lose a few of the delicate nuances during the breading and frying process.

This dish has always been about the combination of the crunchy outer texture and the sweet and gooey inside rather than the quality of the cheese. But I will leave that up to you.

Serves 8

Cranberry Sauce

250g fresh or frozen whole cranberries
60g caster sugar
1 orange, peeled and chopped (use the peel too, but no pith please, we're British – and no pith-taking, either…)
50ml water
5g cornflour, mixed with 1 tablespoon water to make a slurry

Panne

70g(ish) plain flour
3 eggs, beaten
150g dried breadcrumbs (Japanese panko are best for an even finish)
200g round of brie

Assembly

vegetable oil, for deep frying

CRANBERRY SAUCE / Place the cranberries, sugar, orange flesh and peel and water in a pan over a medium heat for about 3 minutes, until the mixture is boiling and the cranberries start breaking down. Add the cornflour and water mix and boil for another minute, which should thicken the sauce. You can keep the sauce chunky, or blend it to a smooth dip. I prefer it smooth for better dippage. Leave to cool.

The sauce can also be used as a relish for turkey and duck, or maybe even venison. Or use it in a pudding, with cheesecake or on ice cream. Oh, the versatility!

PANNE / Place the flour, beaten egg and breadcrumbs in separate shallow bowls. Cut the brie into manageable wedges and roll them first in the flour, then in the beaten egg and then in the breadcrumbs. This is the classic panne breadcrumbing process.

ASSEMBLY / Heat the oil in a deep-fat fryer set to 180°C and fry the wedges for about 3 minutes, until golden, crisp on the outside and molten beneath. Serve the fried brie with lashings of the tart (and cranberry bitter) sauce, be it smooth or chunky.

Scrumpets of Lamb

A scrumpet is a traditional British breaded lamb finger. I have used lamb breast for this recipe, a rather long-lost cut of meat. Try eating the lamb breast without the crumbs, too; it makes for a lovely slow-cooked alternative, whether rolled or left in a slab, falling apart and delicious.

This dish is traditionally made with lamb, but it could also be lovely with veal or pork, maybe even stretching to beef or chicken thighs.

Serves 4,
with a few for the freezer, too

Scrumpets
50g salt
3 sprigs of thyme, chopped
3 sprigs of rosemary, chopped
3 garlic cloves, roughly chopped
1 bay leaf, chopped
1 teaspoon crushed black peppercorns
1kg unrolled, boned lamb breast
vegetable oil

Panne
70g(ish) plain flour, seasoned with salt
    and pepper
3 eggs, beaten
150g breadcrumbs (Japanese panko
    are best for an even finish)

Assembly
vegetable oil, for deep frying
Caper Mayonnaise (see page 169),
    to serve

SCRUMPETS / Mix all the marinade ingredients together – salt, thyme, rosemary, garlic, bay leaf and peppercorns – and sprinkle half of it over a non-reactive tray. Put the lamb on top, then sprinkle over the rest of the marinade. Cover and marinate in the fridge for at least 4 hours, or overnight if you can. This seasons the meat and flavours it with the aromatic herbs and spices.

The following day, preheat the oven to 120°C/100°C Fan/Gas Mark ½. Remove the lamb from the fridge and thoroughly wash off the marinade. Cover the lamb with vegetable oil, a thumb knuckle deep, in a deepish baking tray and cover with baking parchment. Wrap tightly with foil and cook for around 5 hours, until the lamb is tender and falling apart.

Discard any serious gristle, then remove the meat gently from the oil and place it on another tray lined with baking parchment. Cover with a second sheet of parchment, then top that with a tray to weigh it down. You want the lamb to cool down, set and compress. If you can refrigerate it overnight, all the better.

Once cold, the lamb will be hard. Take it out of the tray and cut it into fingers, ready for breadcrumbing.

PANNE / Place the flour, eggs and breadcrumbs in separate shallow bowls. Roll the fingers in the seasoned flour, then in the egg wash and then roll in the breadcrumbs. Any uncrumbed trimmings can be made into a lovely lamb stew. Or just bread everything – all the neat fingers and the odds and ends. At this point the lamb scrumpets can easily be frozen.

ASSEMBLY / Preheat the oven to 200°C/180°C Fan/Gas Mark 6.

Heat the oil in a deep fat fryer set to 180°C and fry the lamb for a couple of minutes, or shallow fry until golden. Transfer to a baking tray and pop into the oven for 5 minutes or so, to warm through in the middle.

Serve with caper mayonnaise and a pint of warm bitter in a heavy dimple mug.

Turkey Escalopes (and Other Relatives) with Cranberry Sauce

Pork, chicken, veal and especially turkey make for a lovely breaded escalope. A wonderfully simple supper, but it may create a slightly smoky kitchen with lots of hot oil everywhere.

Cut thinly and then batted (or is that battered?) out even thinner between some double thickness cling film or those fancy silicone baking mats using a rolling pin. Breaded, shallow fried and served hot with some Cranberry Sauce (see page 88), or perhaps a fried egg, or something strong and salty like anchovies and capers, and always a wedge of lemon.

Serves 4

Panne

70g(ish) plain flour, seasoned with salt and pepper
3 eggs, beaten
150g breadcrumbs (Japanese panko are best for an even finish)
4 x 120g turkey escalopes, cut thinly and further flattened by your rolling pin at home (you can also use chicken, veal or pork)

Assembly

vegetable oil
Cranberry Sauce (see page 88), to serve
a salad of some description (see pages 16–23), to serve
lemon wedges, to serve

PANNE / Place the flour, eggs and breadcrumbs in three separate shallow bowls. Dip the escalopes carefully in the seasoned flour, then in the egg wash, and then finally roll them in the breadcrumbs.

ASSEMBLY / Heat a thin layer of vegetable oil in a wide frying pan over a medium heat (you don't want them to brown too quickly on the outside) and shallow fry the escalopes for about 3 minutes on each side, until golden. If you do them one by one, place them on a baking tray and flash them all in an oven at 180°C/160°C Fan/Gas Mark 4 so they are all hot together.

Serve with a little cranberry sauce and perhaps a posh potato salad, or one of the other funky salads in the book. However you decide to serve it, always include a wedge of lemon.

Cow Pie

I opened my first pub in 2010. It was a fairly alien environment to me – I have never been particularly interested in drinking, especially that famous English warm, flat beer. I wasn't into darts. Not really any good at quizzes. And certainly not into grimy, sticky floors, or eager barmen in checked shirts and ripped skinny jeans calling me 'mate'. Having grown up professionally in fancy, high-end, ambitious restaurants, it took a lot of humble lip-biting on my part to work in a pub kitchen, with a warped floor, an oven bought from eBay and pint glasses of knives, forks and paper napkins on the bare wooden tables.

A life lesson I have learnt since is that some things come through design, whereas others come through opportunity, and this was one of life's opportunities. I suddenly had my own pub, was going to make a go of it and try to adapt.

The most striking thing for me in my new environment was that I had never really considered the social and community aspect of the Great British pub. And I fell in love with it. I love the idea of looking after people, and fine dining is all too much of a show sometimes, and often not so far from the master and servant dynamic that this country has been trying to shake off over the years. Much of what I love about the restaurant industry is connection: connection through food and drink and personal hospitality. Occasionally that is lost in restaurants, with the chefs and waiters having no connection to the food they are making, nor the people they are serving it to.

There is also the problem of expectation. In a restaurant, people expect a certain thing, a certain way, at a certain level, at a certain price. And expectations can sometimes get in the way of having a great time. In pubs I saw that things could be different. If I cooked food at a good level, being wary of alienating any demographic, I could connect in a real way with a far broader audience. And expectations? Well, there wouldn't really be any. I could 'blow the bloody doors off' and excite, delight and captivate people with unexpected touches, from the bread you are welcomed with to the chocolates you leave with, and everything in between.

And so we come to the Cow Pie. This is the dish that now defines my approach to cooking professionally. It fits a number of categories: it is fun, it is skilful, it is delicious, it is direct, it is intricate, it is deceptively simple, it is a great one to eat alone, but better to share, it is proudly British, and accessible to everyone who eats it. It is as relevant and meaningful to the foodie as it is to the unadventurous. In name, it is actually most famous through the cartoons of *The Dandy*, and has been Desperate Dan's staple dinner since the 1930s.

This is a now a bestseller for us, come rain, snowdrifts or that occasional British sunshine. It actually started life as the ultimate leftover dish: piles of unordered beef from an unsuccessful Sunday lunch, with surplus ale from the pub, covered in some simple and traditional suet pastry. The only modern luxury was the bone in the middle; those same bones that they used to give away at butcher's shops as a treat for the dogs, and now a trendy nose-to-bone-and-tail cut that has made this the most expensive part of the whole dish.

It goes very well with a nice warm pint of bitter in one of those heavy dimpled glasses. And don't be overwhelmed by the length of the recipe: it comes in several parts, all of which can be frozen separately, if desired, to spread the preparation. Please bear with it, the results are certainly worthwhile.

BEEF AND ALE STEW / Preheat the oven to 220°C/200°C Fan/Gas Mark 7.

Season the diced beef and pop it in a single layer on a baking tray or two with some vegetable oil and brown in the oven for 20 minutes.

Put the sugar and balsamic vinegar in a wide, deep ovenproof pan over a low heat, add the baby onions and caramelise slowly, moving frequently for about 15 minutes. Take everything out of the pan and set aside.

In the same uncleaned pan, add the sliced onions and mushrooms, and stew with half the chopped thyme and the butter, seasoning well, until they are soft and starting to release some of their natural juices. Add the baby onions back in at this stage, then add the flour and cook out for 5 minutes; it should become thick and gloopy. Add the ale and chicken stock, and mix well to remove any lumps (you can re-jig the ratios of ale and stock to suit availability and taste).

Bring this mixture to the boil, making sure it is not sticking to the bottom of the pan, and re-season with salt, pepper and a little Dijon mustard. Don't forget that this will all be reduced, so don't add too much seasoning at this stage.

Reduce the oven temperature to 150°C/130°C Fan/Gas Mark 2. Add the browned beef and any juices to the pan and put the whole thing in the oven, covered with a lid. Let it cook like a good old-fashioned casserole for 3 hours or so.

When the beef is tender (we call it fork-friendly), check on how thick the sauce is at this stage. If the sauce is too thick, just add a little water, but more often than not it is not thick enough – you're looking for it to coat the back of a wooden spoon. If it needs thickening, scoop out and set aside the tender meat (if left in it can break up and you want it chunky). Make a little beurre manié (equal quantities of butter and flour mixed together to form a paste – in this case, 100g of each). Place the pan over a medium heat on the hob, whisk in a bit of this paste and the sauce should thicken up magically to the perfect consistency.

Then you have to fix the taste of the sauce. Add the remaining thyme, with salt and pepper to taste, and perhaps a little more balsamic vinegar for a sweet and sour element – never forget a bit of acidity in the seasoning.

Return the reserved meat to the pan and leave to cool. You can freeze it at this point if you like. On its own, the stew can be eaten with boiled potatoes on a cold autumn night, or with rice and a few added kidney beans for an exotic twist. But persevere with this here Cow Pie project if you can.

continued on page 98...

Serves 8 hungry cowboys (the component parts of this recipe freeze really well separately, or you can freeze the constructed pie)

Beef and Ale Stew

2kg diced chuck/brisket/shin really are best, or other stewing beef

vegetable oil

1 tablespoon caster sugar

3 tablespoons balsamic vinegar, plus extra to taste

150g baby onions (or use those bulbous spring onions)

250g sliced onions

250g halved button mushrooms

25g chopped thyme

125g butter, plus an extra 100g for the beurre manié (optional)

150g plain flour, plus an extra 100g for the beurre manié (optional)

570ml ale

1 litre chicken stock

2 tablespoons Dijon mustard

salt and freshly ground black pepper

Modern British Food

MARROW BONES / Soak the bones in iced water to firm up the marrow and then pop out the marrow with the back of a wooden spoon. This can then be diced and used in the stuffing recipe below.

Bring the bones to the boil in a large pan of water and cook them for a good hour. Leave them to cool, then scrape off the excess gristle so that you have beautiful clean bones to use as your pie raisers. These can also be frozen at this point, if desired. The leftover 'bone broth' is very on-trend and could be used as a base for stocks, stews or soups – things shouldn't go to waste!

MARROW STUFFING / Blitz the cooked shallots, parsley and breadcrumbs in a food processor to form a green-coloured breadcrumb. Pour into a bowl and mix in the diced bone marrow by hand. Season with salt, pepper and Dijon mustard. At this stage the stuffing can be frozen.

SUET PIE PASTRY / Mix the flour, salt, suet and butter together in a bowl, then pour in the water gradually until you have a dough with little lumps of butter and flecks of suet running through it. Try not to overmix – you still want to see the fat running through it. Place the dough in the fridge until required, or it too can be frozen at this point.

Or you could just use shop-bought puff pastry instead. Less convincing for a cowboy, though.

ASSEMBLY / Select a dish, or individual dishes – not too deep or the pastry will brown and the filling will not be hot enough. You also want the bones to poke through the top like chimneys (4cm deep is best). Arrange the bones, one in each dish for individual pies, or a few in the bigger dish for shared pies, and then put the meat stew around the bones (about 220g per portion if using individual dishes, a cowboy portion) (1).

Roll out the pastry and egg wash the rim (2), and place over the whole lot with a little hanging over the edge (3). Feel where the bones are and press the pastry down over the bones so that they pop through. You may need to use a knife to help, but you should end up with bones poking through the pristine pastry (4). Press the pastry down around the edge of the pie dish and tuck it under any rim. Egg wash the top of the pie and you are ready to go (5). At this stage you can keep the pie in the fridge for a couple of days.

Preheat the oven to 180°C/160°C Fan/Gas Mark 4. Put the pie in the oven for a good 15 minutes, until golden. At this stage you add the marrow stuffing. Take a small handful and shape it into a truncheon (6), bigger at one end than the other, then stuff the smaller end into the top of the marrow bone with the bigger end sticking out. Fill all the bones and return to the oven for 5 minutes or so, until the stuffing is warmed through.

Take the pies out of the oven and serve with some silky mashed potatoes and green vegetables, perhaps a pint of Old Hooky – or (cleverly) the same ale you used to cook your meat. What goes around comes around…

Marrow Bones

6 x 5cm marrow bones (get your butcher to cut these)

Marrow Stuffing

15g roughly chopped shallots, cooked
15g parsley
40g fresh breadcrumbs
200g diced bone marrow – if you don't have enough, make up the rest with diced butter or any other bone marrow
Dijon mustard

Suet Pie Pastry

340g self-raising flour
15g salt
125g suet
90g butter, diced into small pieces
175g very cold or iced water

Assembly

1 egg, lightly beaten

Fish (or Chicken!) Pie

Inspired by the famous Cornish stargazy pie, which has pilchards poking out of the egg and potato filling beneath a pastry crust, this dish will make even the most serious foodie crack a smile. You can make it in smaller individual dishes, or make one big pie with the fish tail popping out of the centre.

Everyone has a favourite fish pie recipe, and this is mine. The filling is simple, classic and comforting, but controversially the topping is a golden puff pastry lid rather than mash, and the presentation is quirky, fun and unexpected. But why-oh-why does everything have to have a twist on it, Jesse, they always say? Well, this might seem like rather a serious amount of ingredients for such an essentially simple dish, but roll with it, and you will be rewarded by a fun and delicious fishy feast for everyone to remember!

(I love pies so much I've even given you an extra recipe here for my favourite chicken pie.)

Serves 6–8

Fish Pie

1 tablespoon vegetable oil
120g butter
2 shallots (or onions, if you prefer), sliced
2 leeks, finely sliced
500ml fresh fish stock
175ml white wine
50g plain flour
200ml double cream
handful each of chopped chives, parsley and tarragon
grated zest and juice of 1 lemon
250g smoked haddock, cut into 3cm chunks
250g white fish, cut in 3cm chunks (try whiting or pollock)
250g salmon, cut into 3cm chunks (you could also use prawns)
3 hard-boiled eggs, chopped
250g block puff pastry
1 egg, lightly beaten
chopped thyme
1 small fish tail (such as sardine, trout or mackerel – ask your fishmonger to help, he might throw you some scraps), to garnish (optional)
salt and freshly ground white pepper

FISH PIE / In a large pan, heat the oil and butter, add the shallots and leeks and cook until transparent, but not browned, about 5 minutes.

Meanwhile, in a separate pan, bring the stock to the boil with the white wine.

Add the flour to the shallot mix and cook for 2 minutes, stirring, but do not allow it to brown. Slowly add the hot stock, stirring continually to prevent any lumps forming. When all the stock has been added, cook over a low heat, stirring occasionally, for about 5 minutes. Remove from the heat and stir in the cream. Cover the surface with parchment paper and leave to cool completely. This can be done the day before you want to serve.

Add the chopped herbs, lemon zest and juice and raw fish to the cooled sauce, stir and season well with salt and white pepper.

Pour the fish and sauce into a deep ovenproof dish (about 30 x 20cm), adding the hard-boiled eggs on top. Roll out the puff pastry and cut a hole in the middle, big enough to fit a fish tail. Lay the pastry on top of the dish, sticking it to the rim with plenty of egg wash. Egg wash the top and chill for at least an hour in the fridge.

Preheat the oven to 180°C/160°C Fan/Gas Mark 4.

Egg wash the whole puff pastry top again, perhaps sprinkle a bit of rock salt and some chopped thyme on top. Stick the fish tail in the hole in the middle of the pie (wrap it with a piece of foil so it doesn't burn) and bake for 30–40 minutes, until golden on top and piping hot inside. Set aside to rest for 5 minutes.

Serve with vegetables such as purple sprouting broccoli, minted peas or buttered carrots.

continued on page 101…

CHICKEN PIE / In a large pan, heat the oil and butter, add the shallots and leeks and cook until transparent, but not browned, about 5 minutes.

Meanwhile, in a separate pan, bring the stock to the boil with the white wine.

Add the flour to the shallot mix and cook for 2 minutes, stirring, but do not allow it to brown. Slowly add the hot stock, stirring continually to prevent any lumps forming. When all the stock has been added, cook over a low heat, stirring occasionally, for about 5 minutes. Remove from the heat and stir in the cream. Cover the surface with parchment paper and leave to cool completely. This can be done the day before you plan to serve.

Add the chopped herbs, lemon zest and juice and chicken to the cooled sauce, stir and season well with salt and white pepper.

Pour the chicken and sauce into a deep ovenproof dish (about 30 x 20cm). Roll out the puff pastry and cut a hole in the middle, big enough to fit a chicken drumstick. Lay the pastry on top of the dish, sticking it to the rim with plenty of egg wash. Egg wash the top and chill for at least an hour in the fridge.

Preheat the oven to 180°C/160°C Fan/Gas Mark 4.

Egg wash the whole puff pastry top again, perhaps sprinkle a bit of rock salt and some chopped thyme on top. Stick the chicken drumstick in the hole in the middle of the pie (wrap it with a piece of foil so it doesn't burn) and bake for 30–40 minutes until golden on top and piping hot inside. Set aside to rest for 5 minutes.

Serve with vegetables such as purple sprouting broccoli, minted peas or buttered carrots.

Chicken Pie

1 tablespoon vegetable oil
120g butter
2 shallots (or onions, if you prefer), sliced
2 leeks, finely sliced
500ml chicken stock
175ml white wine
50g plain flour
200ml double cream
handful each of chopped chives, parsley
    and tarragon
grated zest and juice of 1 lemon
750g diced chicken thigh or breast,
    either cooked leftovers or raw
250g block puff pastry
1 egg, lightly beaten
chopped thyme
1 cooked chicken drumstick (optional)
salt and freshly ground white pepper

Jellies

various forms and flavours

Sweet

The Joy of Custard

Among the philosophy books, the classic novels, the well-thumbed cookbooks and the third-generation children's books with half the pages missing, there was always that rather risqué book, *The Joy of Sex*, by the aptly named Alex Comfort, on the family bookshelves in our sitting room. It was a naughty secret for my little brother and I to flick through, all those long-winded descriptions and the sketched saucy illustrations. But adhering to that phrase 'No Sex Please, We're British', let's talk about something a little more safe and a lot more British: custard.

In Italy it's called 'zuppe Inglese' (English soup!)

Quite how I should link the aforementioned book to a cookbook and a chapter on custard is anyone's guess, but as a proud Englishman I quite like most things with custard. And what better than to dedicate a whole chapter to it, and my unbridled joy of the stuff. Hot and cold, thin and thick, rich and light, runny and set, custard really does have it all.

Now I love a Continental brûlée as much as the next man, and I love a crème caramel too, but I also have a special fondness for a taste of home – be that a tub of Bird's Custard, or even better, a nutmeg-dusted custard tart, both of which will always be firmly associated with England for me.

In fact, so associated with Mother England is it, that custard in France is called 'crème Anglaise', while in Italy it's 'zuppa Inglese' (English soup), and the Italians couldn't be more right with their comparison. Most Brits would be happy with a big steaming bowl of the stuff.

Custard is the wonderful marriage of milk and/or cream, eggs and more often than not sugar. Like mayonnaise, it is a beautiful balance and mysterious union of fairly simple ingredients, greater than the sum of its parts. Textures can vary, with more or less of certain elements, different cooking methods and different partners to marry it with, but all variations rely on the same three or four simple ingredients. Beauty in simplicity.

hot!
custard &
crumble

apple ?

quince ?

rhubarb ?

pear ?

Baked Almond Custard

I love custard, and the introduction to this chapter should make it clear how much exactly. And as much as I love crème brûlée and crème caramel, I wanted to make it a little more British, so I mixed the two dishes and put liquid caramel on top of the custard and gave it some familiar British flavours. This could be infused with almonds (or any nuts), or it could be flavoured with the alcohol and spices of an Eggnog which I love, if a bit grown up. (I've given you both options below.) It just as well could be plain or vanilla'd as well.

It's great served with the crispbreads below or some of Granny Angela's Shortbread (see page 179) or if you are too lazy, get a packet of gingernuts from the local corner shop!

Serves 6

Caramel Topping
200g caster sugar

Almond Crispbreads
50g egg whites (approximately 2 large eggs)
pinch of cream of tartar
60g caster sugar
100g plain flour
150g whole blanched almonds

Almond Caramel Custard
75ml milk
550ml double cream
75g toasted flaked almonds
60g caster sugar
110g egg yolks (about 6 or 7 yolks)

OR

Eggnog Caramel Custard
75ml milk
550ml double cream
30g caster sugar
30g dark brown soft sugar
1 vanilla pod, scraped of seeds, and the empty pod thrown in too
15ml spiced rum
1 cinnamon stick
½ teaspoon ground nutmeg
110g egg yolks (about 6 or 7 yolks)

CARAMEL TOPPING/ Make a caramel: place the sugar in a small pan, add a little water – say 80ml – and bring to the boil over a medium heat. When it starts to turn to a light brown, watch it like a hawk, and when it is dark, very dark and almost burnt (be brave), take it off the heat. Once cool, leave it at room temperature. This should result in a pouring caramel sauce with the texture of runny honey.

ALMOND CRISPBREADS / Preheat the oven to 160°C/140°C Fan/Gas Mark 3. Place the egg whites and cream of tartar in the bowl of an electric mixer with the whisk attachment in place (at the very least use an electric hand whisk), and whisk on high to form stiff peaks. Still whisking, add the sugar slowly and beat until stiff. Fold in the flour and the nuts with a strong wooden spoon.

Spoon into a greased and floured 900g loaf tin, pushing well into the corners – it will come less than halfway up the tin, this is OK – and bake until firm to the touch, about 30–40 minutes. Leave overnight to cool and rest, then slice as thinly as you can with a sharp bread knife and dry out the slices on a baking tray in a low oven overnight at 60°C/40°C Fan, or for an hour at 100°C/80°C Fan.

ALMOND CARAMEL CUSTARD / Put the milk and 180ml of cream in a pan with the toasted almonds and bring to the boil. Place the remaining cream, sugar and egg yolks in a bowl and pour the hot milk over the top. Mix well and leave overnight in the fridge to allow the almonds to infuse into the cream.

The following day, preheat the oven to 150°C/130°C Fan/Gas Mark 2 and strain the mixture into a jug or bowl. Pour this mixture into moulds, perhaps some ovenproof teacups or little ramekins, and place the dishes in a deep tray. Fill the tray with very hot water to halfway up the sides of the dishes you are using. Cover with foil and CAREFULLY put into the oven so as not to spill or jiggle the mixture too much. Cook until there is only a faint wobble on the surface, 30–40 minutes. Take out of the water bath tray and leave to cool, then place in the fridge to set for a good few hours. Serve with the cold caramel poured on top and crunchy almond crispbreads.

EGGNOG CARAMEL CUSTARD / Put the milk and cream in a pan with the sugars, vanilla (seeds and pod), rum and spices, bring to the boil, then remove from the heat and leave to cool and infuse. Refrigerate overnight then follow the recipe above.

Hot Custard
(which luckily can also be served cold)

Bird's Custard is fine, but making your own custard for your own homemade crumble will set you apart from your friends. Real vanilla, real eggs, real cream. Make the full batch even if you don't need it all, I'm sure you'll find use for the leftovers. Serve this hot with your crumble and spotted dick, or cold with a fun-flavoured jelly.

Serves 4

400ml milk
100ml double cream
1 vanilla pod, scraped of seeds, and
    the empty pod thrown in too; plus
    ½ teaspoon vanilla extract, or even
    better that paste you can find in posh
    supermarkets (this is all optional –
    Bird's Custard never had any vanilla
    in it, after all)
50g egg yolks (about 3 medium
    egg yolks)
40g caster sugar
1 tablespoon cornflour

Bring the milk and cream to the boil in a pan with the vanilla, if using.

In a bowl, whisk the yolks and sugar hard until light and creamy, then add the cornflour and stir to combine. Pour half of the boiling milk on to the eggs, whisk together, then pour back into the pan with the rest of the milk and cook it out until it coats the back of a spoon.

Strain out any lumps and serve immediately, or chill down and reheat when needed.

Deep Fried Custard

Deep fried custard might be likened to the best kind of doughnut ever: a bready outer shell filled with 90 per cent custard, rather than a regular doughnut with its 90 per cent dough. I know what I would prefer. What do you think?

Serves 6

Vanilla Slice Custard (see page 110)
70g(ish) plain flour
3 eggs, beaten
150g breadcrumbs (Japanese panko
    are best for an even finish)
vegetable oil, for deep frying
cinnamon sugar
Gooseberry or Cranberry Compote (see
    page 179 or page 88)

Once the custard is cold, turn it out on to a clean board and cut into cubes. Place the flour, eggs and breadcrumbs in separate shallow bowls. Roll the cubes in the flour, then in the egg wash and then roll in the breadcrumbs.

Heat the oil in a deep-fat fryer set to 180°C and fry for a minute or so, until golden. You could also run them through the oven at 180°C/160°C Fan/Gas Mark 4 for a couple of minutes to warm through before serving.

Dust in cinnamon sugar and serve with a fruity compote, or just eat them on their own, hot and sugary lipped.

Vanilla Slice with Blood Orange Marmalade

There are a few specific things that British bakeries ALWAYS stock. Always a sausage roll, always iced buns and always the vanilla slice. The sausage rolls have quite a scary lack of pork in them, the iced buns are normally 95 per cent bun and the vanilla slice only ever has vanilla in the title.

When making this version, pack it with real vanilla, and add that gloopy vanilla paste, if you can find it, to give it an exotic edge.

The French have that famous dish of mille-feuille, which I suppose is the Continental cousin to this dish, and you could go for a thousand layers if you are in the mood, or stick to a more humble two or three.

Serves 4

Vanilla Slice Custard

150ml milk
150ml double cream
25g unsalted butter
50ml water
1 vanilla pod, scraped of seeds, and
the empty pod thrown in too; plus
½ teaspoon vanilla extract, or even
better that paste you can find in
posh supermarkets
50g egg yolks (about 3 yolks)
60g caster sugar
20g cornflour

Caramelised Puff Pastry

300g shop-bought puff pastry, either
in a block or pre-rolled; buy the most
expensive one on offer, it will taste that
much better, and perhaps even have
real butter in it. Puff pastry is one of
those things I have made in my life
(I am a real chef, you know), but I think
it's perhaps best left to others while I
get on with other things
icing sugar, for dusting

Assembly

icing sugar
fruity marmalade or compote – use the
compote recipe on page 179 and use
the julienned zest of blood oranges,
bulked out with the chopped up flesh,
avoiding the pithy white between (or
perhaps ignore all that and make a
blackcurrant, cherry or blackberry
version, which would be just as
deliciously good)

VANILLA SLICE CUSTARD / Bring the milk, cream, butter, water and vanilla to the boil in a pan.

In a bowl, whisk the yolks and sugar hard until light and creamy, then add the cornflour and stir to combine. Pour half of the boiling milk on to the eggs, whisk together and then pour back into the pan with the rest of the milk and cook it out until thick, stirring constantly – this should take about 2 minutes.

Pass it through a sieve, then transfer to a parchment- or cling film-lined tray approximately 25 x 15cm, and chill in the fridge. Only then will it become sliceable. The custard should be about 1cm thick, therefore it is quite important to choose the right tray to chill it in. This needs to be chilled for about 4 hours, or even better overnight to set properly, otherwise it maybe tricky to cut out in the next stage of the recipe.

CARAMELISED PUFF PASTRY / Preheat the oven to 180°C/160°C Fan/Gas Mark 4. Roll out the pastry to a thickness of a pound coin. A little trick with sweet puff pastry is to use icing sugar to dust your rolling surface instead of flour, as it then finds its way into all the pores of the pastry, and when it cooks becomes wonderfully caramelised and delicious.

Cut out pastry shapes about 3 x 4cm. You can stick with the traditional oblong, or go contemporary and wild and cut out round shapes… Think about using two or even three 'slices' of pastry per person, if you can manage – two at the least.

Put the pastry shapes on a flat baking tray lined with baking parchment, with another piece of parchment on top and then another tray on top of that; this way the pastry will stay flat, which is great for the stacking later. Cook for approximately 20–25 minutes, until golden.

ASSEMBLY / Cut out the custard with a cookie cutter or knife, the same shape but just that little bit smaller than the cooked pastry.

Layer the custard, pastry, custard, pastry, and another layer if you are feeling edgy, sprinkle lightly with icing sugar, then scoop and drizzle a little fruit marmalade or compote over and around.

Crème Brûlée Tart with Too Many Flowers

I was inspired to create this dish to celebrate the tradition of the Chelsea Flower Show. I grew up hand in hand with a flowerpot family, the Keelings of the famous Whichford Pottery, and their piles upon piles of terracotta. Their whole year was geared up to 'Chelsea' and, with the show in late May, it was often the first sign of summer, the trailer to the upcoming school holidays.

This is a traditional British custard tart with a makeover: sweet pastry with caramelised custard, covered in a veil of edible flowers. In addition, the custard could be flavoured with a rose syrup or essence, lemon zest or essence, a fruit purée, or an elderflower cordial perhaps, to give it relevance to whatever is scattered on top. Make it your own using whatever you find close by: something abundant, seasonal, clean and beautiful.

Serves 6

400ml milk
100ml double cream
2 vanilla pods, scraped of seeds,
    and the empty pods thrown in too
160g egg yolks (about 8 yolks)
75g caster sugar
15g cornflour
30g plain flour
Sweet Pastry cases (see page 177),
    6 small or 1 large 20cm case
demerara or granulated sugar
edible flowers, to sprinkle – think
    honeysuckle, elderflowers, violetta,
    rose petals, there really are
    many more...

You will need
a blowtorch

Bring the milk and cream to the boil in a pan with the vanilla or any other flavourings (see introduction).

In a bowl, whisk the yolks and caster sugar hard until light and creamy, then add the flours and stir to combine. Pour half of the boiling milk on to the eggs, whisk together and then pour back into the pan with the rest of the milk and cook it out until thick, stirring constantly – this should take about 2 minutes. Pass through a sieve and chill down until ready to use.

Fill the cooked pastry case(s) with the cold custard, scrape it flat and clean on top and sprinkle liberally with demerara or granulated sugar. You want to cover the exposed pastry around the edges with sugar or a little custard too (this tends to burn unless protected). Blowtorch the sugary top until molten and not quite burnt, as you might for a crème brûlée – an industrial blowtorch would really be best, but a little home one might have to do. Leave to cool.

Carefully, but understatedly, scatter edible flowers on top of the cool caramel, so the crust is a surprise. Serve with panache.

Baked Lemon Cheesecake

This is the more traditional of the two cheesecake recipes in the book, and also the more time consuming. The other can be put together in three minutes (I do love an easy recipe).

Traditional doesn't always mean better or more satisfying, but this does have that more cakey, baked texture that people often expect from a cheesecake. So we have a competition: will this baked cheesecake or the quick soft-serve (see page 115) win the cheesecake-off?

Serves 6

Biscuit Base Mix

200g digestive biscuits, or you
   could go wild and use ginger
   snaps or Hobnobs if you're feeling
   'experimental'
60g unsalted butter, melted

Cheesecake Mix

650g cream cheese
100g caster sugar
2 whole eggs
grated zest of 4 lemons (or oranges)
2 teaspoons vanilla extract
cocoa powder or fruity compote (see
   page 179) (optional)

Assembly

Gooseberry or Cranberry Compote (see
   page 179)
fresh berries
Poached Rhubarb (see page 115)

BISCUIT BASE MIX/ In a food processor, blitz the biscuits until fine, then stir in the melted butter and mix thoroughly. Push into a parchment-lined 20cm round cake tin or standard 900g loaf tin until smooth and compact, making sure there are no gaps, especially around the sides. Keep it thin if you can; I hate cheesecakes with an overly thick base. Chill the base until needed.

The Crumble Mix (see page 122) is actually amazing as a cheesecake base here too, if you happen to have some left over.

CHEESECAKE MIX / Combine all the ingredients together in a bowl. If you wanted to add a teaspoon of cocoa powder or a few spoonfuls of fruity purée or compote at this stage – or even to just half of the mix and ripple it – that would work.

ASSEMBLY / Preheat the oven to 160°C/140°C Fan/Gas Mark 3.

Pour the cheesecake mix into the tin to just under the rim (it will rise a bit during the baking). Cook for 30–40 minutes, until it has just a slight wobble. Remove from the oven and leave to cool at room temperature for an hour or so, then place in the fridge to set, ideally overnight. You can eat it fresh, but it will be easier and neater to cut when it is properly chilled down.

Serve a slice with the gooseberry or cranberry compote, fresh berries and poached rhubarb. Once you have tried this one AND the rhubarb soft-serve cheesecake (see page 115), let me know which one is worth the effort – in the preparation and in the eating of.

Rhubarb Soft-Serve Cheesecake

Cheesecake can sometimes be a rather overwhelming and long-winded wonder. Delicious, but requiring some effort, and all sorts of complications can occur. But then cheat recipes come by every now and then and change your life. This is one of them.

One cheesecake mix, in three minutes, using three ingredients, equals a very happy someone who shares this with you.

Marry me for my cheating ways.

Serves 6

Easy-Peasy-Cheese-Cakey

175ml double cream

75g caster sugar

325g cream cheese (Philadelphia is the obvious choice, though Quark works well, too)

flavourings – if you want to get fancy with flavours, try the zest of 1 lemon, or a drop of vanilla extract, or seeds scraped from a fresh vanilla pod, or rose water, or orange blossom water – whatever you like

Poached Rhubarb

125g caster sugar

250ml water

peel and juice of 1 orange

20g piece of fresh ginger, peeled and sliced

200g sliced rounds of rhubarb (about 2 sticks)

Assembly

smashed digestives or ginger snaps (optional)

chopped fruit or berries (optional)

EASY-PEASY-CHEESE-CAKEY/ Place all the ingredients in a bowl and whisk together until thick and creamy. And that is it.

POACHED RHUBARB / Place the sugar, water, orange peel and juice and ginger in a pan over a low heat, bring to the boil, then strain on to the rhubarb in a separate pan. Cook slowly and gently over a low heat until soft but still intact, about 5 minutes or so. Remove from the heat and leave to cool, then strain; you can use the beautiful leftover juice for a jelly or water ice (see pages 118 and 151).

ASSEMBLY / This could be potted, or scooped on to a plate all re/de/constructed like they do on the telly and in fancy restaurants. You could layer it with raw chopped fruit or berries in a glass, serve it alongside some smashed digestives (or ginger snaps for an 'edge'), or garnish it with the wonderful poached rhubarb. And a spoon.

Junket, Jellies and Blancmange

The childhood memories of many people of a certain age and background will include sneakily stealing your own Rowntree's jelly packets and eating square after square, feeling rather ill if you managed a whole pack. Designed for dilution with water into fancy or less fancy moulds, the real treat was to eat the jelly straight from the packet – with or without consent.

Sadly, they only ever managed very pedestrian flavours – orange, lemon and strawberry, among others – but there is the opportunity to try something a bit more fun. Quite why real blackcurrant, elderflower, rhubarb, quince or pear has never made it in the commercial field leaves me a new business proposition to work on. Watch this space.

You could use leftover juice from poaching peaches or pears, or iced tea, chocolate milk, cereal milk, cold Horlicks, iced coffee ... the possibilities are endless. Any liquid can be jellied (although people struggle with pineapple juice because of the acidity, and alcohol always muddles things).

Like the traditional and historic junket and milk puddings of Henry VII's era, thickened with rennet, almonds and boiled calves feet, I often feel that jelly is very British: jelly and ice cream, jelly and custard, forever and ever. This country is also famous for its aspic moulds, and we have them dotted all around the restaurant (yet I struggle to use them correctly, as they are very intricate, need a very hard set to keep the detail, and then need to be turned out of the moulds).

Jelly can be lovely, but it can also be quite underwhelming. The set (using the right amount of gelatine) is key: too soft and you will be drinking the stuff, too much and it is rubbery and unappetising. But also remember the flavour. It must taste brilliant before you add any gelatine. Please don't overlook this.

I love a good jelly, but remember that most gelatine is not vegetarian and the following recipes don't always translate well using the vegetarian alternatives.

As much as I love jellies, I also love a good milk pudding, which is much more British than you might think, but quite plain. It is perhaps inspired by its richer Italian cousin, the panna cotta, the set cream, and sometimes served as a creamy, rich counter to a fresh, fruity jelly.

Serves 6

Jelly*

3 gelatine leaves, if you are brave
    and want a softer jelly; or 1 gelatine
    leaf per 100ml of juice for terrines or
    cakes – have you ever had a layered
    jelly cake…?
500ml juice

* This may vary due to the acidity of the
    liquid, but it generally works as a rule.

**Milk Pudding, or, as the fancy call it,
    Panna Cotta**

3 gelatine leaves
250ml milk
70g caster sugar
flavourings – try herbs, spices, boiled
    bananas, any of the suggestions in
    the introduction, or even some of the
    ideas from the Arctic Roll (see
    page 153).
250ml double cream

JELLY / Soak the gelatine leaves in a bowl of cold water for a couple of minutes.

Warm about 100ml of the juice in a small pan. When very hot, but not boiling, remove from the heat, squeeze out the soaked gelatine and add to the pan. Stir to make sure it is well dissolved, then strain on to the rest of the cold juice.

Think about how it will be served: use teacups, glasses, jelly moulds, shot glasses; you could layer jellies of different colours and flavours (but you must make sure each layer is set before topping with another); perhaps the jellies are turned out, perhaps they stay in the mould you have set them in; you could set them in a tub and scoop out to serve, or even place them in a piping bag and pipe into serving bowls. Pour the liquid into your chosen moulds and refrigerate until set.

MILK PUDDING / Soak the gelatine leaves in a bowl of cold water for a couple of minutes.

Bring the milk to the boil with the sugar, add your chosen flavourings and leave to infuse off the heat for a few minutes.

Squeeze out the soaked gelatine and add this to the boiled milk, stirring to make sure it is well dissolved, then strain through a sieve on to the cold cream. Stir well, pour into the desired moulds and refrigerate until set.

  Modern British Food

Lazy Lemon Pudding

My interest in cooking started at the age of eighteen. Having left school with no culinary skills whatsoever, basic survival was my main aim, so I started cooking simple dishes to keep myself alive. Now, as a fully formed and mature adult, I find it so strange that cooking is not more central to the national curriculum.

To do my part, every week I take a chef from the restaurant and baskets of carefully weighed out ingredients and teach the kids at the local primary schools some cooking. They're not quite ready for the Cow Pie recipe (see page 95), so I usually start with something a little easier. The Soda Bread (see page 176) goes down well, and while that is baking we do something even more simple for them to take home.

Puddings are always a winner, and quick and easy ones like this give lots of pleasure. It's a miraculous little recipe to have up your sleeve, and is called the lazy lemon pudding because even someone as lazy as you can make it. Boil the cream, add a couple of ingredients, and put it in the fridge.

Serves 4

300ml double cream
40ml lemon juice, about 2 lemons, plus their grated zest
grated zest of 1 orange (optional – if you are feeling exotic)
100g caster sugar
digestive biscuits or Granny Angela's Shortbread (see page 179)

Bring the cream to the boil in a pan over a low heat with the lemon juice and zest and, if using, orange zest. Take off the heat and stir in the sugar, followed by the lemon juice. Pour into a teacup or four, then place in the fridge for 3 hours to set.

Serve each teacup on a saucer with a teaspoon and eat with digestive biscuits from the corner shop, or for a bit more quality and excitement, make your own shortbread.

Gooseberry and Elderflower Eton Tidy

Made into a famous mess by a famous school. Made into a seasonal and organised pudding by Parlour under a bit of my OCD direction. Sounds a blast.

Use the ingredients to create a neat and tidy dessert yourself, or just look at the photo (see page 125, bottom right) and follow our lead. A bit of elderflower jelly and gooseberry compote around and about, with a few fresh gooseberries on top of the scoop of cream.

And remember: you can always revert to the classic Eton Mess combination of strawberries, meringue and cream – just make it neater and tidier.

Serves 6

Elderflower Jelly
2–3 gelatine leaves
330ml diluted-to-taste Elderflower
   Cordial (see page 181)

Elderflower Meringue
110g egg whites (about 3 or
   4 large eggs)
pinch of cream of tartar
220g caster sugar
8ml white wine vinegar
10ml neat Elderflower Cordial (see
   page 181)
30g cornflour, sifted

Assembly
Crème Chantilly (see page 181)
Gooseberry Compote (see page 179)
fresh elderflowers – see if you can find
   some in season (June/July)
fresh gooseberries – see if you can find
   some contrasting pink ones

ELDERFLOWER JELLY / Soak the gelatine leaves in a bowl of cold water for a couple of minutes.

Warm about 100ml of the diluted cordial in a small pan. When very hot, but not boiling, remove from the heat, squeeze out the soaked gelatine and add to the pan. Stir to make sure it is well dissolved, then strain on to the rest of the cold cordial. Transfer to a piping bag or a tub and refrigerate until set.

ELDERFLOWER MERINGUE / Place the egg whites and cream of tartar in the bowl of an electric mixer with the whisk attachment in place (at the very least use an electric hand whisk), and whisk on high to form stiff peaks. Still whisking, add the sugar slowly until the mixture becomes thick and glossy. When it is stable and ready (thick and glossy and able to hold its shape), gently fold in the vinegar, cordial and cornflour by hand so as not to break down your careful meringue. Either pipe into cute turrets or scoop into lumps – some small, some larger or all the same neat and uniform at around 6cm diameter – on a parchment-lined baking tray; try and make them tidy if you can – that is what this dish is all about.

Bake low and long, let's say 80°C/60°C Fan for 45 minutes, until crisp outside and fluffy within. Amazingly, they keep indefinitely, which is lucky as there will be lots left over.

ASSEMBLY / You have free rein on how you plate this up, but the rules are that it must be NEAT and TIDY. Have a look at the photographs for inspiration – you have a few elements with which to make it look lovely. Your dining guests are the ones to make it into a right old mess.

Crumble and the Sunday Traditions (PS. Custard, Cream or Ice Cream?)

I love a crumble on a Sunday, and although people might think it is acceptable on any day of the week, I really think you should respect tradition and save yourself for one of England's great Sunday treats.

My dear mama (as well as many others) uses fruit, sugar and raw crumble mix, and bakes it all together, which most of the time, with the benefit of experience and understanding, is fine. But I like a bit more control, so I cook the elements separately, bringing it all together in the oven; fewer soggy crumble issues and more consistency with the fruity filling, I find.

People are very opinionated about food, and some are especially particular about what to serve with their crumbles. I love custard, and will always plump for this. But when offered ice cream, it is difficult to ignore. And cream – firstly, is it pouring or whipped? Although actually, to be honest, I could take it or leave it. You fight among yourselves on this first-world dilemma.

When a lovely young South African sous chef suggested a Sunday lunch menu with banana and maple crumble as a dessert, I kind of understood where he was coming from – he even made one for me and it was lovely – but is it appropriate? Sadly not. It got me thinking about the boundaries of a crumble. Here is a little guideline for you.

Fruit well suited for crumbles, encouraged and traditional:

plums

apples and pears with some vanilla or cinnamon (should you add raisins? No!)

berries, including the Great British gooseberry (one of my favourites)

rhubarb

stone fruit – peaches, nectarines, apricots

fresh figs – I have never tried these, but imagine they might be lovely, if not totally native

Fruit that might sound like a great idea, might well have been tried in the past, but won't go down well in this great country of ours:

grapes

bananas

mango and papaya

melon

oranges

kiwi

pineapple

Serves 6

Crumble Mix
90g salted butter, softened
50g demerara sugar
50g clear honey
180g plain flour
90g ground almonds

Assembly
your chosen compote (see page 179) –
    if it is warm, all the better
Crème Chantilly (see page 181)
Hot Custard (see page 109)
Cheat's Vanilla Ice Cream (see page 180)

CRUMBLE MIX / Preheat the oven to 160°C/140°C Fan/Gas Mark 3.

Place the butter and sugar in a bowl, then add the rest of ingredients, running the mixture through your fingers to form a crumbly dough. Transfer the mixture to a baking tray and cook for about 20 minutes, stirring throughout, until crunchy, toasted and golden (without stirring it will set into a block). While this is cooking it will make your whole kitchen smell wonderful – of toasted honey, almonds and baking! Divine it is, and one of my favourite smells.

This is great to have to hand in your kitchen store cupboard; it will keep at room temperature for a good few weeks.

ASSEMBLY / Both the filling and topping can be made ahead of time and the crumble assembled just before you need it. You can serve the crumble in individual pots, or for a bit more connectivity around the table use a large ovenproof serving dish.

Preheat the oven to 160°C/140°C Fan/Gas Mark 3.

Fill your chosen dish(es) with your chosen compote (or cooked fruit), add the crumble topping, and bake for around 10 minutes, until it is toasty and golden on the top, bubbling around the sides and hot in the middle. Serve with the crème chantilly, hot custard and cheat's ice cream; make sure you have all the crumble accoutrements to hand – you really don't want to upset anyone.

Tarts, Pies and Toasted Teacakes

Us Brits do make a good pie. We also make a good tart. But quite when a pie turns into a tart, or a tart into a pie, is the start of many a long-winded and rather heated discussion. A few disgruntled nit-pickers have in fact pointed out that 'officially' our 'dish to be defined by', the Cow Pie (see page 95), is not a pie because of its lack of base and all-round coverage. It is in fact a casserole with a pastry lid. Rather less alluring, I would say.

And given that a lemon meringue pie is a pie, and a fish pie or shepherd's pie is also a pie, surely there has to be room for some manoeuvre and interpretation? Shepherds and fishermen don't seem to have access to pastry, unless you use my Fish Pie recipe (see page 99), and then we are nearly safe.

The authority on our beautiful and complex language, the *Oxford English Dictionary*, defines a pie as 'A baked dish of fruit, meat or vegetables, typically with a top or base of pastry'. However, my sixth edition of the *OED* describes a pie as 'encased in or covered with pastry'. And rather confusingly, the online version says a pie 'frequently also has a base and sides'. Meanwhile, according to the excellent *Oxford Companion to Food* (no relation to the *OED*, but solid none the less), the meaning of the word pie has evolved over many centuries and varies according to both country and region. I think I will go with that.

And if you thought pies were divisive, you should try that other Great British tradition: the teacake. Some may describe it as a small yeasty bun, perhaps with raisins; some may even stretch to a crumpet being a teacake, while others may say anything drunk with a cuppa is a teacake. But where does that leave Tunnock's Tea Cakes? How do they fit in to all of this?

A traditional toasted teacake is a non-crossed-hot-crossed-bun-type-thing, with a few ye olde British spices, some chopped dried fruits and candied peel perhaps, halved and toasted over a coal fire in the sitting room, using that classic Victorian household implement the 'toasting fork'.

> Yet far away in a distant land the Aztecs went off and invented chocolate, while the Ancient Egyptians were busy creating marshmallows…

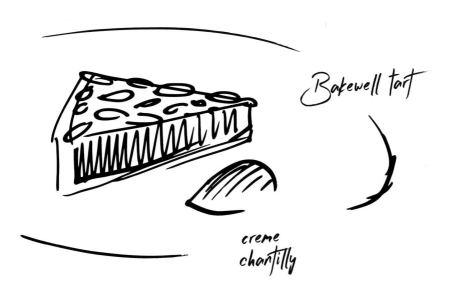

Bakewell tart

creme chantilly

And then it is buttered, always buttered.

Yet far away in a distant land the Aztecs went off and invented chocolate, while the Ancient Egyptians were busy creating marshmallows, and in 1956 the Tunnock's Tea Cake was born in deepest darkest Scotland, to challenge all those teacake traditionalists – radicals and revolutionaries, they really were. Suddenly, biscuits covered in marshmallow and chocolate were the new things to eat with your elevenses.

Weston Wagon Wheels arrived around the same time, and then the Americans tried to get in on the act by going one step further and deconstructing the dish. Leaps and bounds ahead! They invented the DIY toast-your-own, new-wave teacake: a marshmallow s'more.

I have taken elements from the Tunnock's Tea Cake, the Wagon Wheel and the s'more and come up The Parlour Wagon Wheel (see page 135), which is brilliant even without a cup of tea. I will leave you to squabble between yourselves on the intricacies of the English language, but I do love its evolution, and if we can all add our five cents to the mix, by sticking rigidly to what we believe in our hearts, the debate will bubble on.

Battenberg

Serves 15 (you are making two cakes here, to achieve the chequerboard effect, hence the larger serving quantity, but thankfully it keeps well and freezes brilliantly)

England really does have some beltingly good cake recipes in its national archives. In fact it wouldn't be too outrageous to say that we have built the entire nation on a strong cup of tea, plain biscuits and simple cakes.

Yet you only need to venture down the bakery aisles of your local supermarket to see packet upon packet of cakes and biscuits that used to be delicious and well-crafted, but which are now shadows of their former selves. Luckily, I am here to resurrect some of the long-lost memories of tastes gone by.

People love the idea of a Battenberg, but the reality is never that satisfying. I for one am certainly in the camp of no marzipan, please. But this stuff, well, this is what marzipan is supposed to taste like and is really rather life-changing. In fact this cake as a whole will totally change your outlook: a REAL battenberg, with REAL marzipan, made with REAL almonds and a REAL almondy cake – though still with the addition of some less-than-real food colouring. With regards to food colouring, it is always best to use the more expensive gels or pastes rather than the sometimes watery bottles of colour. When baking, it is important to remember that the colours often fade a little from when you first put them in.

And there are two camps when it comes to colour. Either be gentle and make it 'natural looking' or when cooking kitsch classics like the battenberg and Arctic rolls, really go for it and go garish, don't hold back, they certainly didn't back in the 1970s when these dishes were invented.

Makes 2 cakes

Real Marzipan

90g caster sugar

140g icing sugar, sifted, plus extra for kneading and rolling out

225g ground almonds (if making chocolate marzipan, substitute 10g of the almonds with cocoa powder)

1 egg, beaten

½ teaspoon orange or lemon juice

food colouring (optional) – if you really want to add to the drama of the cakes, even the marzipan could have a touch of help in the food colouring department (note, different food colourings are different strengths, so you will have to use your eye to judge the amount you need for your chosen colour)

Cakes

350g unsalted butter, softened

350g caster sugar

280g self-raising flour

100g ground almonds

1 teaspoon baking powder

6 medium eggs

1 teaspoon vanilla extract

½ teaspoon almond extract (optional – you could leave this out for some purity; I prefer without)

yellow and pink food colouring (as noted above, different colourings have differing strengths, so use your own judgement as to how much to use, and remember that sometimes pink colourings fade once cooked)

REAL MARZIPAN / Mix the sugars and ground almonds in a large bowl and rub together until you reach an even texture. Make a well in the centre, then tip in the beaten egg and juice, and, if using, a little food colouring, and mix well. Bring together with your hands.

Dust the kitchen surface with icing sugar, then knead the marzipan briefly into a smooth dough. Don't overdo it as it can become greasy; add a little more icing sugar if it seems too wet. Shape into a ball, then wrap in cling film and keep in the fridge. This can be made up to 2 days in advance.

CAKES / In a large bowl, beat all the ingredients (except the food colouring) together in no particular order – by hand or using an electric mixer.

Place half the mix in a separate bowl and add YELLOW colouring; add PINK colouring to the other bowl. Or you can experiment with colours and do some funky stuff – go wild and do a chocolate and orange version, or plum and custard, or honey and almond, using suitable colours for these flavour marriages. The actual flavours (barring the cocoa version – add a teaspoon or two of cocoa powder at this stage if you are using this) can be added at a later stage with the jam.

Preheat the oven to 160°C/140°C Fan/Gas Mark 3.

Grease and flour two standard 900g loaf tins and pour the separate mixtures into their own tin. Bake until a skewer inserted into the centre comes out clean – depending on your oven this should be 40–50 minutes.

Rich and moist is the almondy way.

ASSEMBLY / Trim the edges of your cakes if they're a little discoloured. Cut your cakes lengthways – one cut top to bottom and one cut side to side – into four square-shaped lengths. If you are feeling adventurous, you could cut them into nine lengths: three cuts top to bottom and three cuts side to side (1 & 2). (If you have any trimmings at this stage, keep them for a trifle – they're brilliant with some sherry, cold custard and whipped cream in a glass.)

Divide the marzipan in two and roll the pieces out so they are big enough to reach around the cakes – you don't need to wrap the ends, just the sides. (It's best to do this on baking parchment or cling film to stop the marzipan from sticking to the surface as you roll, and this will help you shape it around the cake.) Cut the rolled marzipan fairly neatly and slightly warm the jam or chosen spread before using it to slather the marzipan. This will be your culinary cement to help with the construction.

On each jammed marzipan piece, start layering the chequerboard cakes, changing the colour with each step (3). You can go for simple four-step cakes, or go all out for the nine-step special effect … I dare you!

Wrap the marzipan around to cover the sides of the cake, using the cling film or parchment to help stretch it without cracking (4 & 5). Trim or stretch the marzipan over the join and then miraculously hide and seal it with a few firm brushes of a smooth wet knife (6). Trim either and end re-wrap tightly in cling film and leave in the fridge to rest.

Cut carefully, perhaps with the cling film on to help keep everything in place, then take the cling film off each slice (7). Serve with Chantilly cream, and if you have any extra marzipan lying around, roll them into little balls to serve alongside the finished cake.

Assembly

apricot jam or marmalade, or your chosen flavoured jam, or honey, or chocolate spread (see The Parlour Wagon Wheel, page 135)… This is when to add your chosen flavourings – just remember that any dark jam will bleed into the pale sponge and marzipan. Faire attention!

Crème Chantilly (see page 181), to serve (optional)

The Classic Bakewell Tart and Variations

Bakewell tart is the most famous of the almondy, raspberry tart combinations, from the village of Bakewell in Derbyshire.

Like all good well-worn and weathered recipes, it is fairly simple to make, a hardy 'keeper', but what you may not know is that it is also beautifully interchangeable with different nuts and flavoured jams or spreads. Some lovely options include:

pistachio and cherry
peanut and chocolate spread
hazelnut and blackberry
walnut and grape jelly

Serves 8

100g butter
100g caster sugar
100g eggs (about 2 eggs), beaten
100g ground nuts – almonds or other
    whole nuts ground in a coffee grinder
    or food processor – anything goes
Sweet Pastry cases (see page 177),
    8 small or 1 large
1 egg yolk, beaten
jam, classically raspberry (WITH seeds
    please), but let your imagination run
    wild on this one
chopped or flaked nuts
apricot jam, for glazing
crème fraîche or soured cream, to serve

Cream the butter and sugar together in a bowl, by hand or using an electric mixer. Add the eggs slowly, followed by the ground nuts. This mixture is best used cold (though not essential), so you could make it a few days in advance and store in the fridge. It even freezes well.

Seal your cooked pastry case(s) with a lick of egg yolk to make sure they don't spring a leak, then spread a thick layer of your chosen jam in the bottom of the shell(s).

Preheat the oven to 170°C/150°C Fan/Gas Mark 3.

Cover the jam with the nutty filling and sprinkle with flaked almonds or perhaps walnut halves, or wait until it is cooked to sprinkle with smaller chopped nuts.

Cook for 25–30 minutes, until puffed and golden and a skewer inserted into the centre comes out clean. Leave to rest for a good 30 minutes–1 hour; this is best served at room temperature.

Once it's cooler, warm a little apricot jam until it is runny and loose, then paint the top of the tart to give it a lovely sheen. If using smaller chopped nuts, sprinkle them on at this stage, and serve with the crème fraîche or soured cream.

The Parlour Wagon Wheel

When I was young, school dinners were all about packed lunches, with sandwiches cut rather too thickly, soggy from the filling, some rather hippy-ish dried dates, perhaps some grapes and, if Mum was feeling flush and we deserved a treat, a Club biscuit or a Penguin Bar, or, if all the planets aligned, a Wagon Wheel.

There has been much controversy about the wagon wheels that we serve. Regardless of whether people love them or not, and aside from them not being totally true to the original recipe – that much I can take – diners often try and catch us out about the jam. 'Where is the JAM!?' they shout.

Well, actually, the jam is only in the blue-packet Wagon Wheels; those in the red packets are without jam, so we are going to stick with serving red ones. Then there is the famous American campfire treat of the s'more: a particular brand of biscuit (the Graham cracker) with bonfire-toasted marshmallow and a wedge of fatty American chocolate that doesn't taste of much. Not only does it look handsome and mostly taste good too, but the performance and the delivery of it is sometimes the only reason people actually order it. For it is flamed 'tableside' as the Yanks would say. Not flambéed (as the French might do), but flamed, by the waiter and an industrial blowtorch. It is quite something.

I remember the first time we ever blowtorched something in front of a customer, and I watched on the CCTV as the nervous waiter approached the table to a nervous punter, neither quite knowing what was going to happen or how each other was going to react, or in fact the outcome. It ended well on both sides and we have gained such confidence since that even the floppy ginger-haired apprentice waiter Matthew is now entrusted to scare the three-year-olds with the brandishing of his welder's torch on an innocent marshmallow, much to the excitement of the children and often the shocked surprise of the parents.

We have taken inspiration from both the wagon wheel and the s'more, and with an added theatrical presentation of blowtorching the marshmallows in front of startled children we have come up with a winner! Lovely cookies, chocolate spread, homemade marshmallows and a dash of pizzazz.

Sometimes cooking is just about holding your breath and trying something new. Making marshmallows was exactly that for me, as I was always slightly overawed by them – little did I know that they really are hardly more difficult to make than an Italian meringue. And I am so glad I discovered how to make them with a little zest through them, or flavoured with vanilla or cocoa powder – even chopped nuts work really well. They can be dipped in chocolate, or made in a tray and cut up as brilliant edible presents. Push yourself today, go on!

Each element is worth making on its own, but put them together and the planets really do align, making all the effort worthwhile.

Serves 6

Marshmallows

100ml water

1 tablespoon liquid glucose

225g caster sugar

60g egg whites (about 3 eggs)

pinch of cream of tartar

5 gelatine leaves, soaked in 70ml water
    for a couple of minutes

50/50 cornflour/icing sugar mix,
    for dusting

Wagon Wheel Cookies

80g caster sugar

90g soft dark brown sugar

90g butter, softened

1 egg

140g chocolate chips, chopped by hand
    or finer in a food processor

150g plain flour

½ teaspoon salt

1 teaspoon bicarbonate of soda

1 teaspoon vanilla extract

Wagon Wheel Chocolate Spread

140ml double cream

40g soft dark brown sugar (the darker
    the better)

50g dark chocolate, chopped

Assembly, you will need

a blowtorch

MARSHMALLOWS / Heat the water with the glucose and caster sugar in a small pan until it reaches 127°C: watch it closely as it gets near the magic 127 number.

At the same time, place the egg whites and cream of tartar in the bowl of an electric mixer with the whisk attachment in place (at the very least use an electric hand whisk), and whisk on high to form stiff peaks.

Once the sugar mixture hits 127°C add the soaked gelatine and any remaining soaking water, stirring and whisking in well, then slowly pour this sugary gelatiney mix into the fluffy egg whites while still whisking on high, and leave it whisking until it starts to thicken and cool for about 15 minutes or so. This will allow the mixture to be thick and glossy and hold stiff peaks.

When it is cooler and very thick, transfer it to a piping bag and pipe little marshmallow kisses, as big or as high-peaked as you dare, onto trays lined with baking parchment. Put them in the fridge for an hour or so to chill properly.

Once cold and firm, remove them from the tray and dust all over, including the base, with the cornflour/icing sugar mix. Put in an airtight container and keep in the fridge.

WAGON WHEEL COOKIES / Preheat the oven to 160°C/140°C Fan/Gas Mark 3.

Place the sugars and butter in a bowl and cream together by hand or using an electric mixer. Add the egg, along with the chopped chocolate, flour, salt, bicarbonate of soda and vanilla extract, and stir until well combined.

Roll out the cookie dough between two sheets of baking parchment so it's the thickness of a pound coin, and bake for 12–15 minutes so they're still soft. It is actually better to cook the mixture as a whole sheet and, once cooked, cut the cookies out while still warm and then leave them on the sheet to cool – this gives a much better edge. You need to cut out 12 cookies, either just rounds, or we go one step further and cut a hole in the middle of each one to make it that much more 'wheel like'.

WAGON WHEEL CHOCOLATE SPREAD / In a pan over a low heat, bring the cream just to the boil with the sugar, then remove from the heat and fold in the chopped chocolate. This needs to be chilled to reach the desired spreadable thickness.

ASSEMBLY / Allow two cookies per person (to make a sandwich), and cover each with the chocolate spread, then cover one of the cookies in marshmallows. Blowtorch the marshmallows and then squash the two sides together. There you have it: a toasted marshmallow wagon wheel. But of course.

Kosher Black Pudding and Other Chocolate Relatives

A good few years ago I was offered a London exclusive of dried camel's milk, with all its supposed brilliant health benefits and delicate nostalgic Arabic nuances. It was a new one for me, but being brave and spirited I bought 2kg from my misguided friend Simon, who took the money and ran. I made panna cottas from it, to a muted reception. I made ice cream, to a similar response. And then I made Arctic rolls from it, calling the dish Camel-ised Arctic Roll – a bit of mystery and intrigue – and luckily the waiting staff got behind it (with a twinkle in their eyes) and even sold a few portions. I wouldn't call it a runaway success by any means, and I still have about 1.5kg in a dusty box in the back of the dry store somewhere if anyone wants some.

> It was a new one for me, but being brave and spirited I bought 2kg from my misguided friend Simon, who took the money and ran.

Simon came back several years later with a new business proposition: Lithuanian chocolate, called Chocolate Naive, which was also a new one for me. It was named 'Naive' because of the Lithuanian chocolate maker who once lived the high life of a glamorous London City banker, only to give it all up to return to his home country and produce chocolate for discerning London chefs. (Still) being brave and spirited, I bought 2kg from Simon, who took the money and ran. I have been using it ever since.

Although the chocolate is grown elsewhere, it is turned from bean to bar in Lithuania, and the Naive Lithuanians have some lovely products, including 100% cocoa chocolate – bitter, grown-up and a brilliant counter to salted caramel and other sweet marriages.

I love my chocolate, mostly for its variety and versatility – think soufflés, mousses (or even mooses), spreads, ice creams, sorbets, tarts, wafer thin mints... And catering as we often do to the north-west London Jewish community, I thought we would add a particular treat for them,

chocolate
moose
?!*

so we started making Kosher (Chocolate) Black Pudding (see page 147). Luckily the joke is still as funny as it was the first time. Instead of pigs' blood, fat and spices, think chocolate, fruit, nuts, biscuits and (Kosher) marshmallows. It has been a mainstay of the menu in one form or another, and is actually more familiar than it may at first seem, being a take on rocky road or the classic chocolate fridge cake or tiffin.

Try some of these recipes, and perhaps even try them with different chocolates – use different percentages, and even dip down into the lowly milky stuff. The same dish can be elevated into something else entirely with a carefully considered chocolate.

Hot Chocolate Tarts

A molten-centered, chocolate pastry-lined tart. It might just be what dreams are made of. Serve them with some cheat's ice cream (see page 180) or some simple crème chantilly (see page 181).

Really this is best made as small individual tarts, as the mixture is essentially undercooked and therefore runny inside, unless you choose to cook it through for a big tart and slice it. (This is just as tasty, just not quite as lip-smackingly sensual!)

Serves 4

100g dark chocolate
100g butter
100g caster sugar
30g plain flour
100g egg whites (about 3 large eggs),
   raw and unbeaten
4 small Sweet Pastry cases (see
   page 177)

Melt the chocolate and butter together, either in a microwave or in a bowl over a pan of simmering water (make sure the bowl is not touching the water). Off the heat, add the sugar, flour and finally the egg whites, and stir to combine. It's as easy as that.

Preheat the oven to 180°C/160°C Fan/Gas Mark 4.

Fill the cooked pastry cases with chocolate mix – 80–90g of filling is usually enough for a portion inside the individual shells. Alternatively, this mix could be cooked without the pastry case, in ovenproof teacups or ramekins. Cook until there is a slight wobble still on top, about 8–10 minutes. If you slightly undercook the mix it will be soft-centred and amazing, but it still tastes nice when cooked through. Eat straight away, hot from the oven.

  Modern British Food

100% Chocolate Pot

When a successful and driven young man working in the world of international finance in London decided to give up the good life to return to his native Lithuania to make chocolate, his whole family said he was incredibly naive – so naïve that he named his company after it. And it has been a wild and tasty success ever since. Chocolate Naive is the best 100 per cent cocoa solids chocolate I have ever had; it has real flavour, very little sweetness, and is great for cooking with.

Another super easy recipe, rich and indulgent, this mixture could even be poured into a pre-baked pastry case (see page 177) and served as a chocolate tart.

A grown-up pudding, I would say.

Serves 4

300g dark chocolate (the 100% stuff, if you can find it), chopped
120ml milk
300ml double cream
2 eggs

Place the chocolate in a bowl set over a pan of simmering water (make sure the bowl doesn't touch the water) and melt until it's HOT to the lip.

Boil the milk and cream together in a pan and pour on to the eggs. Whisk well, or use a stick blender to combine. Add this mixture slowly to the chocolate, little by little, incorporating it as it goes, whisking at first, then stirring in with a spatula.

Pour into glasses – if you can find some, try those lovely open-faced coupette glasses, sometimes called a 'Marie Antoinette' glass (legend has it, moulded on her perfect little B cups). Or if you really must, use ramekins or normal little water glasses. Leave to set in the fridge to firm up for an hour or more, then remove about an hour before serving, so they can soften up at room temperature.

You could serve them with a dollop of crème fraîche or soured cream on top to resemble caffè macchiato, alongside some of the almond crispbreads (see page 108) or some shortbread (see page 179), and possibly a real hot, dark caffè macchiato.

Alternatively, you could pour the chocolate mixture into a large cooked sweet pastry case (see page 177) and leave to set in the fridge for a couple of hours. Slice it while cold and serve at room temperature so it is beautifully soft.

DTC's Salted Caramel Chocolate Rolos

Dave the Cook (actually christened David Cook) has worked with me a few times in different kitchens over the years. Regardless of his consistently inconsistent timekeeping, he always adds something to the business before he leaves – a legacy, some may call it. Dave certainly had lots to do with the beginnings of this dish, so much so that we named it after him posthumously. (Just to be clear, he didn't actually die, I just haven't heard from him in a while. And DTC is, obviously, Dave the Cook.)

For this recipe you need to try and source some chocolate casings: hollow chocolate spheres with holes in the top for filling. I have seen these for sale in posh sweet shops, so you might need to make a trip to a chocolatier (which are also all the rage these days).

Crisp chocolate, gooey caramel and salt – a wonderful combination. Mackintosh's have done a wonderful job with the classic Rolo since the 1930s, but they left out the salt flakes. Guess we've improved on a classic. You be the judge. I like to serve an uneven portion, leaving an awkward last one in the bowl at the end. Who has been good enough to deserve the last rolo?

If you add a little more cream to this recipe it turns into a beautiful sauce for vanilla ice cream. French it up a bit and you have the much more romantic-sounding sauce *caramel au beurre sale.*

Makes 40 (far too many, but then again you don't want to run out, that would be tragic; they keep well, so it's not a problem)

200g caster sugar
50g butter
150ml double cream
5g Maldon sea salt
dark chocolate truffle shells
200g dark chocolate (the darker the better – 60% at least if you can't track down 100% stuff; it's a great contrast to have a bitter shell with sweet caramel inside), for rolling
cocoa powder, for rolling

Make a caramel: place the sugar in a small pan, add a little water – say 80ml – and bring to the boil over a medium heat. When it starts to turn to a light brown, watch it like a hawk, and when it is dark, very dark and almost burnt (be brave), take it off the heat, pop in the butter and stir it around. BE VERY CAREFUL – it will foam up and splutter, so stand back. Add the cream, little by little, and stir it in well. Once incorporated, leave to cool, and ONLY once it is cool, add the sea salt. Keeping it at room temperature, stir the caramel well to incorporate any salt that may have fallen to the bottom, then place the caramel into a piping bag and pipe into the chocolate casings, getting them as full as you can. Leave in the fridge to set for an hour or so.

Place the chocolate in a bowl and melt in a microwave, for 20 seconds at a time, stirring after each blast until melted (or go old-school and melt it in a bowl over a pan of simmering water). Let it cool a little, then dab the chocolate case openings with a fingertip of melted chocolate to seal in the caramel (you could fridge them again at this point, but it's not necessary). Dab one of your palms with some melted chocolate and your other thumb and index and middle fingers too, and, one by one, roll the filled chocolates in your hand to lightly coat them in chocolate, and then throw them into a bed of the cocoa powder. They will set once they hit the cocoa.

Return to the fridge to allow the caramel to set and to firm up the outer chocolate coating. Your hard work will be rewarded with beautiful chocolates that will keep for quite a while, but I doubt they will survive that long. Any excess caramel is great set aside for a rainy day, when effortless joy is needed.

Light Chocolate Mousse

Everyone has a favourite family chocolate mousse recipe, and if you don't have one, here it is. This is best made with the darkest chocolate you can find (see page 138 for the story on 100 per cent Lithuanian chocolate), but can also be made with milk, or even white chocolate, if you have a VERY sweet tooth.

This is another of those recipes where you can make it your own. Sometimes I have served people with a big bowl of mousse and a spoon and lots of little pots of different sprinkles: hundreds and thousands, Smarties, cookies, honeycomb, fruity sauce or compote (page 179), popping candy, rolos (page 145), dried fruit, nuts, chopped chocolate pieces, crumble topping (page 122) chopped white chocolate … the list goes on. If you are as funny as me – unlikely I am sure – you could also serve with a bit of crunch, such as wafers, and there is a recipe below. This can be shaped into anything, make a little mould/stencil and off you go; you could make your chocolate mousse into an equally delicious and but also side splittingly funny chocolate MOOSE.

Serves 6

Mousse

50ml milk

grated zest of 1 orange (you could also use a few pinches of coffee beans, 1 tablespoon Horlicks, even a little peanut butter…)

75g dark chocolate (the darker and higher the percentage, the better; you could use milk chocolate, or even white chocolate, but it gets very sweet)

180ml double cream

75g caster sugar

40g egg yolks (about 2 yolks)

Simple Tuile Mix

50g icing sugar

50g egg whites (about 2 medium eggs)

50g plain flour

sprinkle of cocoa powder, chopped hazelnuts/almonds/walnuts, food colouring (optional)

MOUSSE / Bring the milk and zest (or your chosen flavouring) to the boil in a pan, then remove from the heat and leave to cool and infuse for about 5 minutes.

Place the chocolate in a bowl and melt in a microwave for 30 seconds at a time, stirring after each blast until melted (or go old-school and melt it in a bowl over a pan of simmering water), then strain the infused milk on to the chocolate and stir to combine.

In a separate bowl, whip the cream with the sugar until soft peaks form, then add the yolks and combine gently. Fold this carefully into the chocolate mix, then transfer to a piping bag or tub to set in the fridge for a few hours. It may look a little soft, but it will set in the fridge.

SIMPLE TUILE MIX / Preheat the oven to 160°C/140°C Fan/Gas Mark 3. Combine the ingredients in a bowl to make a paste. This is a classic wafer mix – you can make as much as you want; just use equal quantities of the ingredients.

If you want to get funky and creative with the colouring, now is the time. Personally, I would stick to brown for a more convincing 'moose'. You can use cocoa powder or food colouring, even chopped nuts to sprinkle on top.

With the back of a spoon, spread the mixture into funny shapes on a silicone baking mat; if you are clever you could fashion a moose-shaped plastic template and spread the tuile mix over it with a flat spatula. Cook for 8 minutes, or until golden (make sure the fan doesn't blow the silicone mat around in the oven). They will look cooked, but will still be soft and will only crisp up as they cool.

Serve a scoop of mousse with a funky shaped tuile for moosey effect, and possibly a little caramel sauce left over from DTC's Salted Caramel Chocolate Rolos (see page 145).

Kosher (Chocolate) Black Pudding

I'm not sure if the Jewish hanker after a slice of black pudding, but they don't have to wait any longer. It's not treif – it's safe.

Some call it chocolate fridge cake, others rocky road. We shape it to look like a fine *boudin noir*. It could be served on its own with a cuppa, or as part of a dessert such as the Light Chocolate Mousse (see page 146) to give it an edge or a bit of a lift.

This is a great recipe, easily tailored to your own loves and whims by adding pretty much anything:

nuts – think pistachios for a bit of colour, or a mix of different nuts

dried fruits, apricots, cranberries and figs, as well as the classic raisins and sultanas

marshmallows – not too big

small sweets like Maltesers and Smarties

Turkish delight

cereal – Rice Krispies, Shreddies, the choice is yours

broken biscuits

white chocolate buttons or pieces

Serves 6

100g butter
150g golden syrup
60g cocoa powder
300g mix of nuts/raisins/broken biscuits/ marshmallows (see introduction)

Melt the butter and golden syrup together in a pan over a low heat, add the cocoa powder, then fold in the other bits. This could be pushed into a cling film-lined loaf tin or springform cake tin, or if you want it round and looking like a black pudding, you must learn to do the cheffy cling film roll and shape it into a sausage.

Create your desired shape, then place in the fridge for a few hours to firm up. Once cold, it's better to keep the cling film on while slicing for a cleaner cut and remove before serving (for the sausage shape).

Serve slices with whipped cream, ice cream, or just as an after-dinner treat with coffee.

Wafer Thin Mints

I love Monty Python so much that I begged my wife to call our first-born Monty. She half-relented at a weak moment while expecting twins, saying that 'If there was a boy, we might call him Monty.'

We didn't find out the sexes before my wife gave birth, so we were always going to have a bit of a surprise. During childbirth, however, things didn't go exactly to (my) plan, and we didn't have a boy for our first-born. We got a girl instead. Luckily we love dear Ada now. Initially I was quietly disappointed, and prayed for the second coming. Miraculously, we had a boy, and as dreams sometimes do come true, we called him Monty.

Now, much as I love Monty Python, there is one character in particular who stands out from a scene in *The Meaning of Life*: Mr Creosote. As some of you might remember, he was an incredibly fat man, so fat he only just managed to squeeze himself into the restaurant, before ordering the whole menu, the whole wine list, with a side order of bucket, which he ended up projectile vomiting into for the entire meal.

At the end of the meal, when the waiter asked if there was anything else he could get him, he was met with rather a gruff negative response. Pushed further by the impatient waiter to try a 'wafer thin mint', poor Mr Creosote couldn't help himself and he gave in, accepted the treat, causing his poor overfed stomach to murmur, grumble and strain under the pressure – until it all got a little too much for him. It was the straw that broke the camel's back, and the poor man exploded, covering the waiter, the whole restaurant and all who ate in her. All because of that final treat of the wafer thin mint.

Here is my version of that famous after-dinner mint, chocolatey, strong with mint and with a high dark cocoa percentage. After Eights have never tasted so good.

Tempering chocolate only requires one ingredient, but is rather complicated. This is for the more confident cooks out there, and is less about touch and feel, as some of this book's recipes are, and more about strict, careful and disciplined following of some tight guidelines.

  Modern British Food

Break 300g of the chocolate into a heatproof bowl and set over a half-filled pan of simmering water (a bain-marie). Make sure the bottom of the bowl doesn't touch the water below. Also take care that the water is not boiling too furiously, but just at a simmer. Stir the chocolate all the time to even out the melt.

Finely chop the remaining chocolate and set aside. When the chocolate is melted, but more importantly HOT to the lip (or if you are keen enough to have a thermometer, it should be about 56°C), remove about one-third of the melted chocolate and set it aside in a warm place.

Off the heat, stir the unmelted chopped chocolate into the larger bowl of melted chocolate, making sure it is fully incorporated. This will lower the temperature of the chocolate (it should be lukewarm or cool to the lip; or 28°C on a thermometer). Finally, still off the heat, add the reserved melted chocolate to increase the temperature of the chocolate (again, put a little on a spoon and then put it against your lip – it should be at just under blood temperature; or 32°C on a thermometer). After this whole process your chocolate should be tempered, and when cool should have a shine to it and a good snap.

On some baking parchment or wax paper, or ideally an acetate sheet, pour tablespoons of the melted chocolate into little puddles and work them into neat rounds with the back of the spoon, creating large dark chocolate button shapes. You can also do little ones, fancy, cheffy skid-mark ones, or if you cut a mould out of plastic, you could even go so far as making square ones, like those offered up at posh dinner parties after 7.59pm.

Makes about 40 (plus trimmings)

400g dark chocolate (55% or higher)
1 x 48g packet of Extra Strong Trebor Mints, ground in a coffee grinder to make a minty dust

While the chocolate is still soft, dust each one with a sprinkle of the ground mints (you probably won't need the whole lot – maybe make some cheat's ice cream with the rest, see page 180), then leave them to firm up in the fridge for 10 minutes. Once cold, they will set with a snap, and can be easily removed from the paper and kept in an airtight container until it is time for the bill.

Garçon – a bucket!

Water Ice

Ice cream and even my slightly cheat version (see page 180, in which I reveal some secrets about 'frozen-mousses'), all are fairly complicated to make and require equipment, thought and planning. However, here is a great recipe to make a freezer treat from any delicious sweet leftover roasting or poaching juice, or cooking stock – refreshing and very simple to make. I give you the Great British Water Ice.

Like its cousins, the ice cream and sorbet, you will need to churn the mixture, stirring the freezing ice regularly to produce a crystallised texture; it's just as refreshing, but with a somewhat cleaner taste.

It is great with fresh berries, or countered by some cold custard, set cream or panna cotta hidden at the bottom of a glass and covered in a pile of water ice for contrasting textures, flavours and mouth-feels.

Here are a few ideas of what to make when your newfound love of water ices truly kicks in:

> a fruit cordial (see page 181)
> leftover juice from cooking rhubarb (see page 115)
> fresh lemonade or orange juice, or any fresh juice you have to hand
> your favourite cocktail
> blended stewed fruit; or strain the fruit and just use the juice
> iced coffee or tea

Serves 4

Juice
500ml tasty juice – see intro for ideas
(but really any amount, this is just
a guide)

Assembly
custard component of the Crème Brûlée
Tart (see page 111) (optional)
chopped fruit, to complement the juice
used (optional)

JUICE / Pour the liquid into a non-reactive, flat-bottomed tray or glass dish and place in the freezer for about 30 minutes. It might take a while to get started (more than 30 minutes in the beginning), but you will see it start to freeze after a while. Stir the mixture with a fork and allow it to freeze for another 30 minutes. Repeat this process every 30 minutes for 3 hours or so, making sure the ice crystals around the edge are pushed into the middle.

The water ice will keep indefinitely in your freezer, but may seize up after a certain amount of undisturbed freezer sleep. Just leave it at room temperature for 15 minutes, then start scraping and stirring – it will come back to life.

ASSEMBLY / The water ice is traditionally served ungarnished in a frozen glass, as a refreshing interlude or end to a meal. I like to include some kind of contrasting or relevant partner – some cold custard at the bottom of the glass as a creamy counter balance to the dish, or some fresh fruit covered in the blanket of frost.

Arctic Roll

Makes 2 rolls, each serves 6 hungry Eskimos (with a little leftover for a rainy, or more likely sunny, day)

Surely everyone's favourite childhood pudding?

It could well have a romantic Arctic or even Antarctic heritage, but more likely it was invented in a factory in Milton Keynes by a 'food technician'. Yet no visit to the grandparents was complete without a slice of Arctic roll, back before Werther's Originals were invented. Although sadly the only flavour on offer was the classic vanilla ice cream with raspberry jam and sponge. Things have moved on since then though, in leaps and bounds.

I was challenged, once upon a time, to make this British classic for the famous chef Mark Hix when I helped him open a restaurant in Soho. I made six versions of the classic combination, with thick sponge, thin sponge, rippled jam, unrippled jam, churned ice cream and a frozen mousse. He wasn't very impressed with any of them, shrugged his shoulders and wandered off. Rather despondent, I served them all to a very excited staff table the next day.

Six months later I was cooking 'butch British pub grub' of my own, and while scrabbling around for ideas on classic and nostalgic puddings, thought it might be a great idea to resurrect that aborted attempt at Arctic roll and put my creative spin on it. What better canvas than to be able to mix up different flavours and colours of ice cream, with jam and sponge, and have funny, alluring titles pointing to the familiar and less-familiar.

I always have a rotating roster of at least fifteen flavours of ice cream in my freezer, some more classic than others. They make the most brilliant last-minute-ice-cream-birthday-cakes all piled up, and people can play the game of trying to work out what the different flavours are. The possibilities really are endless!

Like the catchphrase from *Blue Peter* (the show you would probably have been watching the last time you ate this), 'here's one I made earlier', this is a great pudding to pull effortlessly out of the freezer when it is time for afters. And if you are organised, you could even make more than one flavour. I dare you.

The recipe comes in several parts and is fairly complicated, but if you bear with it, the results are worthwhile and will keep indefinitely in the freezer for endless treats.

Previous 'interesting' flavours that we have tried, on top of the more traditional coffee (Nescafé), Bounty, salty popcorn and overripe banana, have been: Aquafresh, Hubba Bubba, Montecristo (yes, the cigar chopped up and infused in the cream), Fisherman's Friend, Thai green curry, basil seed, pea and mint, scented geranium, Rice Krispies, sweet fennel, builder's tea, smoked bacon, Crunchy Nut Cornflakes … and the list keeps growing with the next enthusiastic chef who joins the team.

'Chef, have you ever tried Christmas Tree infused cream…' It went on the menu the following day. Fancy chefs call it Douglas fir; rather like a forest fresh pine loo cleaner, only sweet, fun and some have even muttered 'delicious'.

Here I have given you the recipe for my green Thai curry ice cream, but you could use the Cheat's Vanilla Ice Cream instead (see page 180). (I suggest you start well ahead of time to allow for the freezing time for the various components and assembly.)

Try something new today!

**Green Thai Curry Ice Cream
(or use my Cheat's Vanilla Ice
Cream on page 180, or any ice
cream flavour combination
you fancy)**

500ml double cream (must be cold –
warm cream will never whip, that
much is guaranteed)

20g lemongrass, chopped

40g galangal, chopped

5g kaffir lime leaves

20g lime peel

3g cardamom seeds (about 10)

1 large red chilli, kept whole

15g mint leaves

20g ginger, peeled and chopped

50g desiccated coconut

80g egg yolks (about 4 yolks)

4 eggs

150g caster sugar

food colouring – alongside the flavour,
you may also need to give a visual
enhancement, adding colour to make
it look right. A lot of infused creams
will come out white or beige and
are in need of a little visual trickery.
Supermarket food colouring is fine –
the little 'toothpaste' tubes of paste
are best

You will need

we use cut-off black plastic drainpipes
about 2 x 11inch or 5 x 30cm
(seriously), cling filmed at one end,
and have yet to find a better solution
(see page 155, step 6 for a photo).
Find two lengths of clean drainpipe
that will fit in your freezer, with edges
smoothed

GREEN THAI CURRY ICE CREAM / Boil the double cream together with the lemongrass, galangal, kaffir lime leaves, lime peel, cardamom seeds, chilli, mint, ginger and coconut, and refrigerate overnight to infuse (1).

Surprisingly delish.

Place the egg yolks, eggs and sugar in the bowl of an electric mixer with the whisk attachment in place (or at least use an electric hand whisk) and whisk hard until twice the original volume (2 & 3).

Once infused, either colour a bit of the flavoured cream green or a bit red depending on whether you want Thai green or Thai red curry effect (4).

Fold the flavoured whipped cream slowly into this eggy-sugary base until smooth (5). Pour into the round tube mould or cling-filmed drainpipes (or into a tub for normal scooping) and freeze for at least 5 hours, or ideally overnight (6).

continued on page... 157

  Modern British Food

7

8

9

10

11

12

SIMPLE SPONGES / Place the sugar and eggs in the bowl of an electric mixer with the whisk attachment in place (or at least use an electric hand whisk) and whisk until twice the original volume.

Now, colour can be added to the sponge; if you are using more than one colour, now is the time to separate the mixture into different bowls, one for each colour (7). Make the colour of the sponge relative to the colour and taste of the ice cream it will wrap (it will all make sense, I promise). Here I've used the colours of the Thai flag, as you can see in the pictures (8). Fold in the sifted flour to each coloured mixture carefully, so as not to knock out too much of the air (9).

Preheat the oven to 220°C/200°C Fan/Gas Mark 7.

If using more than one colour, separate each mixture into different piping bags – use a nice big bowl or tin to help you. Skip this step if only using one colour.

Spread the mix out to 0.75cm thick on two parchment-lined trays, so the sponge is big enough to roll up your tubes of ice cream. If using a mix of colours, use the piping bags to pipe a striped effect (10 & 11). Bake for 5 minutes, then remove from the oven and leave to cool. Lay the sponge on a bed of cling film and carefully peel the old baking parchment off (12).

This sponge is also really good for a trifle, tiramisu or Swiss roll. Even a cake with ganache between numerous layers is a fun one. It freezes well, too.

Simple Sponges
100g caster sugar
5 eggs
food colouring
100g plain flour

continued on page 158...

Assembly

jam or other spread, such as chocolate, salted caramel, etc. – classically, raspberry jam is used, but go for any other funky flavour you like. Again, just make sure it's relative to the flavour you are making; apricot jam can be used as a neutral 'glue'

You will need

a blowtorch
a rolling pin

Leave the sponge to cool for a few minutes, then thinly spread jam or your chosen spread all over it (13).

Take your ice cream drainpipe and remove the cling film. To help ease the ice cream out, blowtorch the plastic tube slightly all around, just enough to release the ice cream but not enough to melt the plastic (14). (Alternatively, run the pipe under some hot water to soften the ice cream a little.) Squeeze it out using a rolling pin as a pusher from one end (15). Place the tube of ice cream down the middle of the sponge. Trim the edges of the sponge to the size of the ice cream roll (16), and then use the cling film to help you roll it up (17). Wrap with new cling film and smooth down all the edges. Leave in the freezer for a good few hours, or overnight, to set again. It will keep for a long time wrapped in the freezer. Slice as needed to serve (18).

13

14

15

16

17

18

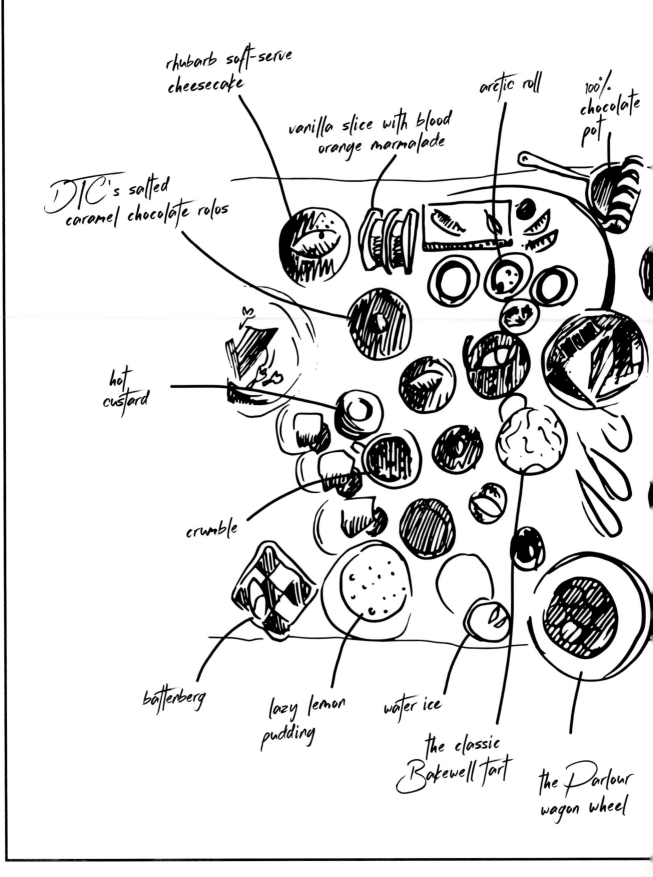

rhubarb soft-serve
cheesecake

vanilla slice with blood
orange marmalade

arctic roll

100%
chocolate
pot

DTC's salted
caramel chocolate rolos

hot
custard

crumble

battenberg

lazy lemon
pudding

water ice

the classic
Bakewell tart

the Parlour
wagon wheel

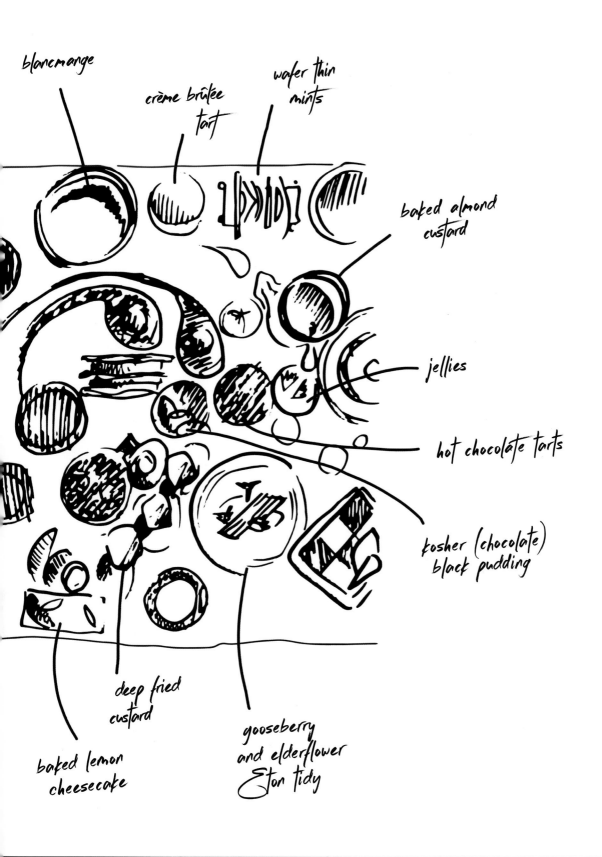

blancmange

crème brûlée tart

wafer thin mints

baked almond custard

jellies

hot chocolate tarts

kosher (chocolate) black pudding

deep fried custard

baked lemon cheesecake

gooseberry and elderflower Eton tidy

Pantry

Ketchup
Apple, beetroot, butternut, tomato, raw and cooked

Ketchup is that favourite side-of-the-plate condiment that brings a dish to life. No wonder our Great Britain is so addicted to the stuff. What we yearn for in this sauce, often without realising it, is the sweet and sour effect – that, and the savoury umami. And having written at some length about acidity on page 34, it all suddenly makes sense.

You can use this as a base recipe, adding cooked or even raw vegetables and fruit (there is a little list below) to achieve your desired taste. Ideally, use a NutriBullet or high-speed smoothie maker to emulsify this properly.

Cooked options (by no means exhaustive): beetroot; apples or pears; pumpkin or squash; gooseberries.

Raw options (these could also be cooked too): mushrooms, tomatoes, peppers, stone fruit (apricots, peaches, etc.).

Makes 1 bottle

200g cooked or raw vegetables or fruit
   (see introduction)
25g Rosemary Sherry Caramel (see
   page 36)
25ml white wine vinegar
100ml vegetable oil
50ml olive oil
½ teaspoon xanthan gum
salt and freshly ground black pepper

Blend all the ingredients together, season and pass through a sieve. This would be great with the gala pie (see page 40).

Houses of Parliament Sauce

Not nearly enough people know that the most famous brown sauce in this country, best served with a bacon or sausage sandwich, and normally referred to as HP, is actually named after our Houses of Parliament, hence the picture on the bottle.

Despite the exceedingly long list of ingredients, it is in fact really easy to make. Put everything together, boil it up, thicken and blend. Your house will smell like an Indian restaurant, however, so try and bake some almond and honey crumble immediately afterwards to counteract it.

The sauce keeps well, and can even be frozen; all that sugar and vinegar certainly helps with the preservation.

Makes 1 bottle (with leftovers)

125g shallots or onions
vegetable oil
250g tinned tomatoes
150g dates, chopped
1 teaspoon ground ginger
1 teaspoon turmeric powder
1 teaspoon cayenne pepper
1 teaspoon coriander seeds
1 teaspoon mustard powder
1 piece of orange peel
5 cloves
5 black peppercorns
100ml water
50g soft dark brown sugar
50g black treacle
250ml malt vinegar
15g cornflour

Gently fry the shallots or onions in a little vegetable oil in a large pan until softened, then add the rest of the ingredients except the cornflour. Bring to the boil and simmer for 30 minutes. Mix the cornflour with a little water (to make a slurry) and add to the pan to thicken the sauce. Remove from the heat once thickened, then blend to a smooth sauce and pass through a sieve.

Serve with sausage rolls, steak and burgers, or alongside a barbecue. It is a lovely thing to have in your pantry.

Mayonnaise
and its many cousins

Makes a good tub

Traditional Mayonnaise

60g egg yolks (about 3 yolks),
    pasteurised if possible (available
    online and in some supermarkets)
15g Dijon mustard
1 tablespoon lemon juice, plus extra
    to taste
300ml vegetable oil
white wine vinegar, to taste
salt and freshly ground black pepper

Spiced Mayonnaise

1 heaped tablespoon smoked paprika
300ml vegetable oil
60g egg yolks (about 3 yolks),
    pasteurised if possible (available
    online and in some supermarkets)
15g Dijon mustard
1 tablespoon lemon juice
salt and freshly ground black pepper

Aioli

Traditional Mayonnaise ingredients
    (see above)
100ml olive oil
3 garlic cloves

Tartare Sauce or Caper Mayonnaise

200g mayonnaise, from the above
    recipe, or use the stuff from a jar if
    you are that lazy
50g chopped shallots
100g chopped capers
10g chopped parsley
2 hard-boiled eggs, chopped (optional
    for the tartare sauce – I love it
    with eggs as they give a good
    richness; omit entirely for the caper
    mayonnaise)
lemon juice, to taste
salt and freshly ground black pepper

Homemade mayo is not as scary as it might first seem. It will also change your life when compared to the shop-bought stuff. It's great to always have in the fridge, and as you can see from this, it's really versatile.

You can add all sorts of chopped herbs or mustards, or make it with flavoured oil (or partially with nut/lemon/chilli oils that you can make or buy). Try not to be tempted to make it with olive oil, as great an idea as it sounds, because it's always much too strong, and often bitter, but you could replace a third of the vegetable oil with olive oil to achieve different results.

Experiment and have some fun!

TRADITIONAL MAYONNAISE / Mix the egg yolks, mustard and lemon juice together in a bowl. Using a stick blender, food processor, electric mixer, or even by hand, God forbid – so many ways to make mayonnaise – add the oil slowly in a trickle. If it becomes very thick, add a little water. Once combined, add more lemon juice, or a little white wine vinegar to sharpen it up (fatty things like this need a good amount of acidity), and a generous amount of salt and pepper, too. This will keep for 5 days or so in an airtight container.

SPICED MAYONNAISE / Warm the smoked paprika in half of the vegetable oil in a pan until too hot to stick your finger in (imagine it…). Leave to cool, add to the rest of the oil, then follow the recipe above.

AIOLI / Substitute 100ml of the vegetable oil for olive oil, and add 3 cloves of very finely chopped garlic to the egg yolk mixture at the beginning, then follow the recipe above.

TARTARE SAUCE OR CAPER MAYONNAISE / Combine all the ingredients in a bowl and adjust the seasoning to taste.

Hash Browns

One of my favourite guilty secrets was McDonald's Hash Browns … I was so happy to discover how to make them myself – they're really not that hard. What more could you want with a couple of fried eggs?

Serves 6

1kg medium-sized potatoes (Maris Pipers work well, or look for the Potato Lovers brand, if you can find them), peeled
1 teaspoon chopped thyme
1 teaspoon salt
vegetable oil

Boil the whole peeled potatoes in a pan of salted water until firm but tender to a knife. Strain and leave them to cool.

Grate the potatoes into a bowl, add the thyme and salt, and mix well. The gluten in the potatoes will make them a little sticky, which for this dish is great. Taste the mix to make sure it has enough salt.

Weigh out 140g balls of the mix and make some hockey-puck-sized discs; squeeze together hard to compact them well. These are now finished hash browns, ready for the cooking stage, and can be kept covered in the fridge for a few days if needs be.

Heat a little vegetable oil in a frying pan and shallow fry the hash browns, keeping them moving, for about 5 minutes on each side, until golden, crisp on the outside and aromatic and mash-y inside.

Celery Salt
(Homemade is always best)

I think of celery salt as proudly British. Traditionally served with boiled eggs, or gull eggs if you are posh enough, you can also pair it with Attenborough's Neolithic Eggs (see page 39) or use it to add an edge and depth to soups, stews and dressings.

More often than not these days, celery is trimmed to within an inch of its life. You sometimes find untrimmed, bushy celery in farmer's markets, and sometimes in Asian supermarkets where they are sold with more leaf on them.

Makes 200g (maybe a little less once dried and blended)

50g celery leaves (the outer and inner leaves from 1–4 heads, depending on how leafy your celery is)
200g table salt

Pick the leaves from the heads of celery and combine with the salt on a tray.

You can leave this in an airing cupboard for a good few days or even a week to naturally dry out. If you want to speed up the process, place the mix in a low oven (about 60°C/40°C Fan) overnight, and in the morning the salt and heat will have dried out the leaves totally, leaving them rigid and crisp.

Blend in a food processor until it comes out a mysterious green-grey. It will keep forever in an airtight container.

House Dressing

Makes 1 bottle

Funk it up, make it your own, add more olive oil, mustard, vinegar or herbs and experiment! This is great in an old wine bottle in the door of your fridge, something you should always have to hand come rain or shine.

100ml olive oil
100ml vegetable oil
50ml white wine vinegar
20ml water
1 sprig of tarragon
1 teaspoon caster sugar
20g Dijon mustard
salt, to taste

Simply whisk all the ingredients together, add a little salt to taste, and preferably leave to infuse overnight before using.

Brine for Chicken and Turkey

Brining your roast chicken (or your simple steamed chicken breast or barbecued drumsticks) will change your life. You will never want to go back to a regular naked chicken ever again. It's the same for turkey (pork chops have their very own recipe – see page 80). If it's cold enough outside, and you can find a large pan or bucket to brine your chicken or turkey in, leave it overnight in the garage or porch. But beware of the dog or the local fox, who may have rather a taste for brined meat. Take precautions.

Bring half the water to the boil in a large pan with the herbs, garlic and lemon peel. Add the sugar and salt, then remove from the heat and add the remaining cold water. Leave to cool completely, then strain. The brine should preferably be used COLD.

To brine a whole chicken or turkey, submerge it in the brine for 4–5 hours (overnight will not be a problem). Make sure it is completely submerged, perhaps using a damp J cloth or even a plate to keep it under the liquid. The smaller the bird, the less time it needs in this tasty bath; for single breast fillets, thighs or drumsticks, a couple of hours would do. Please try and think about the kind of meat you are using: outdoor reared, organic free-range meat is always the preference for me. Let your conscience get in the way of this one.

Makes 1.2 litres

1.2 litres cold water
a few sprigs of thyme
a few sprigs of tarragon
1 bay leaf
1 garlic clove, smashed
2 pieces of lemon peel
70g caster sugar
50g salt

And have a play with the flavour of your brine: use your favourite spices or herbs, for example. Use this recipe as a guide (keep the sugar/salt/water ratio, but most other things can be tweaked).

Once brined, you don't have to wash the liquid off, drip-drying is fine, then cook your meat in the usual way. The brine can be used for a second bath, and could even be frozen to keep for another day.

Self-Raising Flour

Not got quite enough self-raising flour left? Shops closed and you're now stuck in the middle of a recipe with nowhere to go? Worry no longer. This was a revelation to me, and hopefully it will be to you, too.

Makes 1kg

1kg plain flour
50g baking powder (or 25g bicarbonate
    of soda and 25g cream of tartar)

Sift the ingredients into a bowl and mix, making sure there are no lumps. Easy.

Rosemary Pitta

Based on the most simple of chapati recipes that I picked up travelling in India: flour, water, salt. I first made it fairly traditionally, and then I tried it with infused water, then added some parsley and then someone used self-raising flour by mistake and made it better suited to our equipment and kitchen. This is now far from tradition as chapati, or as a real pitta.

They can be made well in advance and fridged or frozen beforehand. Fresh is best but tricky to time. Nothing like pitta straight out of the fire, as it were.

Place the rosemary and water in a large pan, bring to the boil, then remove from the heat and leave to infuse overnight.

Put the flour and salt into the bowl of an electric mixer with a dough hook attached and start to mix. Add 100ml of the rosemary water (if you have failed to prepare in advance, use 100ml water with a little chopped rosemary), until you reach a dough consistency. Then add the chopped parsley and mix again.

Weigh the dough into 75g portions and roll out flat into rounds or the classic oblong or oval shape.

Cook in a DRY frying pan over a medium heat, for 2–3 minutes each side, until coloured on both sides. It should be puffed and pillowy. The pitta can also be made in advance and fridged or frozen.

Makes 10

a few sprigs of rosemary
500ml water
200g self-raising flour
5g salt
10g chopped parsley

Soda Bread

Bread is one of the most important dishes in the world, something almost every nation shares in its own regional way. Don't underestimate the importance of bread at a mealtime. Breaking bread together is biblical, and I like to serve this as a whole loaf to share together at the table, a ritual that signifies the start of a meal and a communal experience.

This also just happens to be one of the most robust and foolproof bread recipes you are likely to find. It is deeply satisfying, sweet, dense, some may even stretch to traditional, although I have had various disagreements with certain Irishmen (and the occasional Irishwoman) about its authenticity. It keeps very well uncooked, and can be pulled from the fridge or freezer and cooked up into a fresh loaf effortlessly.

I can't quite remember how I found the base recipe, but I tinkered with it for a year or so to get to what we have today, and it has remained unchanged for several years.

This is also a brilliant recipe to get the kids involved with, too. I often use it when doing kids' cooking classes at the local primary school, as it's something you can make and bake in real time, and while it's in the oven, there's time to put together another little dish.

**Makes around 6 small loaves
or 1 large**

375g plain flour (I have also made it with brown, wholemeal and even self-raising flour before, with little change to the final product), plus extra for dusting
125g porridge oats
15g salt
15g bicarbonate of soda
30g soft dark brown sugar
375ml buttermilk, or natural yoghurt or milk – even soy milk works for a dairy-free version
50g black treacle or molasses

Mix all the ingredients together in a bowl – in no particular order – and bring together into a ball. Easy as that, it really is.

Preheat the oven to 220°C/200°C Fan/Gas Mark 7 (ideally, cook with low fan or no fan, so the flour isn't blown off).

Form the dough into 6 small loaves or 1 large loaf. Traditionally, they are round and cut deep into quarters. Spray with water, then dust heavily with flour and bake for 18–20 minutes for small loaves and 30–40 minutes for a large loaf, until a deep toasty colour and hollow-sounding when knocked.

The dough keeps very well once made. Make it, ball it and fridge it for up to 5 days, well covered in cling film, then bake when needed. Comes up fresh as a daisy. And delicious, too.

Sweet and Savoury Pastry

Leaving home you really need a good few recipes to arm yourself with to survive the outside world. Luckily I have covered most bases here in this book. Soda bread, salad dressing, simple pasta dish (raw vegetable raviolis don't really count), cottage (or perhaps even cow) pie, simple roasts and brined chicken, steamed fish, carrot and new potato cookery, lemon posset and shortbread to name a few... And perhaps how to make simple pastry such as the recipes below.

Not a survival essential, but when your new in-laws come over, or there is a bring and share wedding that you might need to impress at, bring out the quiche or the chocolate tart and prepare to wow the masses with your fine techniques!

**Makes 1 large 20cm case or
6 small ones**

Sweet Pastry
80g butter
170g plain flour (if making chocolate pastry, substitute 20–30g with cocoa, or to simply funk the pastry up, substitute the same quantity with ground almonds or hazelnuts)
60g icing sugar (caster will work, but won't be so refined)
grated zest of 1 lemon, orange or lime
1 egg, beaten

Savoury Pastry
65g butter
1 egg
250g plain flour, plus extra if necessary
1 teaspoon salt
pinch of sugar
40–65ml water

Assembly
2 egg yolks, beaten

SWEET PASTRY / By hand or using a stand mixer, combine the butter, flour and sugar with the zest. Add the egg and bring the dough together, then cover in cling film and leave to rest for a couple of hours.

SAVOURY PASTRY / By hand or using a stand mixer, combine the butter, egg, flour, salt and sugar together. Add the water as necessary to bring the dough together. If it's too sticky add a little more flour. Cover in cling film and leave to rest for a couple of hours.

ASSEMBLY / Preheat the oven to 180°C/160°C Fan/Gas Mark 4.

Roll out the pastry to the desired size and thickness, then stuff into your chosen rings or moulds. Always remember to push the pastry firmly into the corners, paying particular attention to this for a professional finish. (I prefer to leave the pastry overhanging and then trim it once cooked.) Leave it to rest in the fridge for 30 minutes or so to firm up again.

To blind bake, line the pastry base with ovenproof cling film/baking parchment/foil and fill with dried peas or chickpeas to help support it during the baking. Cook for 20 minutes or so until golden, then remove the peas and lining and return to the oven for 5 minutes or so to finish cooking and brown the base. You can then seal the tart with a lick of paint, an egg yolk or two washed around the inside of the shell to make it watertight.

Nutty Praline

One of the most dangerous, but also one of the easiest recipes in the book. We have used this with various nuts, in various guises, for various dishes, hot, cold, sweet and savoury – you have to admire its versatility. It keeps really well and is a great thing to have in your pantry, or squirreled away in the freezer.

It can be used to lend a sweet and nutty note to a goats' cheese salad, is great sprinkled on ice cream or added to a chocolate mousse for a bit of crunch and earth, or served alongside a soft-serve cheesecake (see page 115), or the Stilton custard (see page 46).

Serves 6

200g nuts – I suggest either the
    traditional almonds or hazelnuts,
    but it has been made with walnuts,
    pistachios, macadamia (if feeling rich),
    peanuts (if not so flush), and even
    pumpkin, sunflower or sesame seeds
100g sugar
50ml water

Preheat the oven to 160°C/140°C Fan/Gas Mark 3.

Toast the nuts on a parchment-lined baking tray in the oven for about 6 minutes or so, until brown and deliciously fragrant, then remove and set aside in a warm place.

Make a caramel: place the sugar in a small pan, add the water and bring to the boil over a medium heat. When it starts to turn to a light brown, watch it like a hawk, and when it is dark, very dark and almost burnt (be brave), WORKING FAST, take it off the heat, add the warm nuts, stir and turn out on to a parchment-lined baking tray IMMEDIATELY, spreading it out thinly so that it cools down quickly. Please re-boil the pan with lots of water in it to get rid of the stuck caramel – it's much better than trying to scrub the pan clean.

Leave to cool for at least 30 minutes; it will be too hot and soft otherwise. Once cool, chop by hand to keep chunky, or blitz in a food processor to form a sweet nutty crumb. This will keep almost indefinitely and, in addition to this recipe, can be used in a number of lovely toppings for salads, meat dishes, but most commonly for puddings – in or over ice cream is LUSH.

Granny Angela's Shortbread

Great Granny Angela's family cooking repertoire only really consisted of shortbread, but what shortbread it was. And thankfully I managed to prize the recipe from her to share with others. This goes well with the lemon pudding, a jelly or even just with a pot of Earl Grey like the old dear used to enjoy.

Makes 1 large tray

300g plain flour
200g butter
100g caster sugar, plus extra
   for sprinkling

Preheat the oven to 160°C/140°C Fan/Gas Mark 3. Mix all the ingredients together by hand or using a stand mixer until crumbly. Push into a parchment-lined cake tin, or onto a lined tray (preferably with a side lip on it), and score for visual effect or so it's easier to divide once cooked.

Bake for about 15 minutes, until golden and toasty, and sprinkle with sugar as soon as they come out. These keep well in a sealed container, and are great served with a lemony pudding, or as a snack with a cuppa for the overworked cook.

Fruit Compote

Gooseberries are great cooked like this and served with cheese instead of a classic chutney; they're lovely with cheesecake (see pages 114 and 115), or even with grilled fish like mackerel (see page 63) – but also try using apples, berries, cherries, or other similar fruit for variation.

Serves 6

Gooseberry Compote
250g gooseberries (or whatever fruit you
   have chosen to stew), ends trimmed
50g caster sugar
grated zest of 1 lemon
50ml water
1 teaspoon cornflour
salt, to taste (if using for a savoury dish)
white wine vinegar (optional – if using
   for a savoury dish)

Simple Apple Compote
500g peeled, cored, roughly chopped
   apples – Bramleys are best for
   stewing, as they break down well
   (pears, plums and rhubarb are great
   cooked like this, too)
100g caster sugar
pinch of ground cinnamon, or a small
   handful of raisins chucked in before
   cooking, or a vanilla pod (even just the
   leftover scraped skeleton)

GOOSEBERRY COMPOTE / Place the gooseberries, sugar, lemon zest and water in a pan over a low heat and bring to the boil. Mix the cornflour with a little water (to make a slurry), add to the pan to thicken the sauce, then remove from the heat once it's reached the desired consistency. You can keep the compote chunky, or blend some or all of it into a smooth purée.

If using this as a savoury accompaniment, add salt to taste, and maybe a dash of white wine vinegar to sharpen.

SIMPLE APPLE COMPOTE / Preheat the oven to 180°C/160°C Fan/Gas Mark 4.

Place the apples, sugar and any extras in an ovenproof dish, cover with foil and bake for about 15 minutes, until the apples have broken down and become soft. Give it a stir and another 10 minutes, if needed.

This can be made in advance and freezes well. It's great with meat, as a dip for crackling or the pork scratchings (see page 48), with yoghurt for breakfast, or as a crumble filling (see page 121).

Cheat's Vanilla Ice Cream

A kind of French-frozen-mousse-thing-translated-as-'perfect': a parfait. Unlike real ice cream, this is not churned, but it's not a bad imitation as it is whipped, trapping air bubbles and making it seem lighter and ice-creamier in some way. Your friends and family will never know otherwise. This cheat's ice cream also reacts well to being put in a Tupperware box and frozen for scooping or slicing.

Serves 6

500ml double cream (must be cold – warm cream will never whip, that much is guaranteed)

3 scraped fresh vanilla pods, or that vanilla paste you find on fancy supermarket shelves, or flavour the cream with whatever you like: you could infuse the cream the day before with herbs (think basil, lemon thyme, kaffir lime, mint); your favourite sweets (jelly beans, chewing gum, boiled sweets, Kendal mint cake, toffee, fudge); fruit or vegetables (zests, boiled bananas, butternut squash, peas); or on the day itself add a flavour such as cocoa, coffee, Horlicks, Ribena, any type of purée, syrup or alcohol – you think of it, we have probably already done it

80g egg yolks (about 4 large yolks)

4 eggs

150g caster sugar

food colouring – alongside the flavour, you may also need to give a visual enhancement, adding colour to make it look right. A lot of infused creams will come out white or beige and are in need of a little visual trickery – make the bubblegum look pink and bubblegummy! Supermarket food colouring is fine – the little 'toothpaste' tubes of paste are best

You will need

cut-off black plastic drainpipes (see page 154) and blowtorch (if for Arctic Roll) or a plastic tub (if not for Arctic Roll)

Whip the cream with your chosen flavouring to soft peaks and set aside somewhere cool. This amount of cream could be split into two to make two different flavours.

Place the egg yolks, eggs and sugar in the bowl of an electric mixer with the whisk attachment in place (or at least use an electric hand whisk) and whisk hard until twice the original volume.

Fold the flavoured whipped cream slowly into this eggy-sugary base until smooth, and add any food colouring. If using two flavours, split the egg and sugar mix into two and fold the creams in separately. Pour into the round tube mould or cling-filmed drainpipe, if using, or into a plastic tub for scooping, and freeze for at least 5 hours, or ideally overnight.

Crème Chantilly

Whipped cream can be a thing of beauty: simple, thick and rich. Crème Chantilly, on the other hand, is something else entirely: light and fragrant. I have never gone back to plain whipped cream having had a real crème Chantilly. It is harder to overwhip, and lighter because of the addition of milk.

To make this a little more funky, try adding some lemon or orange zest. The milk can also be totally or partially replaced with a cordial or purée (elderflower or strawberry, for example), even a glug of some fortified tipple that might go well with what you are serving. Try a chocolate or malted version using cocoa or Horlicks, or even salted caramel, with a few sprinkles of salt on top to finish. Icing sugar is best in this, as it dissolves quickest, but caster sugar is passable, and it has even been made with dark brown sugar for something a little more exotic.

Serves 6

125ml double cream
20ml milk
1 vanilla pod, seeds scraped, and
   the skeleton saved for a custard
   (see pages 108–111)
10g icing sugar

Place all the ingredients in a bowl and whisk until thick. Always err towards underwhipped – you can bring it on to full whip anytime by beating it a little more. This can be made ahead, but over time the whip will fall, and it will need a little extra whipping to lift it when ready to serve.

Elderflower Cordial

This makes about four bottles and is lovely to have at hand. It doesn't go off because of the very high sugar content, but is best kept in a cool pantry, or in a fridge if possible. You can dilute it with fizzy or still water for a refreshing juice, and it is amazing in cocktails. Think also jellies (see page 118), mousses and water ices (see page 151), or as a general addition when cooking (it is the perfect seasonal marriage when cooking gooseberries). Or decant it into smaller bottles for a homemade present.

Alternatively, you could make your own Ribena with fresh or frozen blackcurrants, and I have recently been introduced to a fennel option, because of the abundance of flowering fennel in my father's garden, which was unexpectedly delicious.

Makes 4 bottles

1.1 litres water
2kg caster sugar
75g citric acid
200g heads of elderflower (about 25
   heads), or the flavour options are
   endless: flowering fennel heads;
   blackcurrant leaf (try it); lemon
   verbena; rose geranium; mint; fig leaf;
   400g berries (red ones, black ones
   and even goose ones; frozen work
   really well too); 400g(ish) of apple,
   pear or quince trimmings, peelings,
   cores and otherwise discarded bits
   from another dish
peel and sliced flesh of 3 lemons
sprigs of mint

Heat the water and sugar in a large pan, bring to the boil, then remove from the heat and add the citric acid. If using berries or apple/pear/quince trimmings, add them at this stage. Alternatively, pour the boiling liquid on to the elderflower heads (or the herbs, leaves or fennel flowers), the sliced lemons and lemon peelings. Stir well and cover with cling film. Leave to cool, then transfer to the fridge for 4 days.

Strain it, bottle it and keep it cool until ready to use. For best results, dilute with sparkling water (or if feeling flush, Prosecco), a little lemon peel and fresh mint. Yes please, more please.

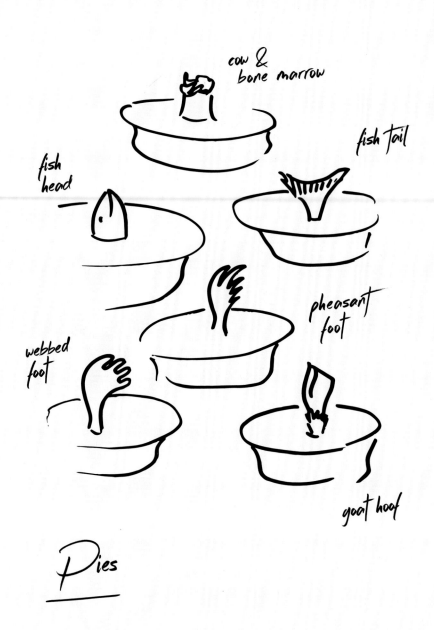

cow &
bone marrow

fish tail

fish
head

pheasant
foot

webbed
foot

goat hoof

Pies

Index

A

aioli 169

almonds
  almond crispbreads 108
  baked almond custard 108
  trout with peppers and almonds 56

apples simple apple compote 179

Arctic Roll 152–9

Attenborough's Neolithic eggs 38–9

B

basil seed dressing tomato and samphire
  salad with peach and basil 20–1

Battenberg 128–33

bean salad with hazelnuts 23

beef
  beef and ale stew 96–8
  cow pie 94–8

bhajis fried onion bhajis 52–4

biscuits
  Granny Angela's shortbread 179
  the Parlour wagon wheel 135–7

blancmange 117

blue cheese
  chicory salad 19
  Stilton custard with walnuts 46–7

brandy duck liver pâté 33

bread
  rosemary pitta 173
  soda bread 176

bread sauce 69

breadcrumbs see panne

brie fried brie with cranberry sauce 88–9

brine for chicken and turkey 172

broad beans bean salad with hazelnuts 23

brown sauce Houses of Parliament
  sauce 168

butters steak with too many butters 78–9

C

cabbage rainbow coleslaw 23

cakes
  Battenberg 128–33
  the Parlour wagon wheel 135–7

caramel 108
  DTC's salted caramel chocolate
    rolos 144–5

carrots
  carrot cooking liquor 69
  fish soup 30–2
  rainbow coleslaw 23

celeriac mushroom 'tea' and hot buttered
  crumpets 28–9

celery salt 170–1

Cheddar cheese
  leek and cheddar tart 49
  onion and cheddar soup 27

cheesecakes
  baked lemon cheesecake 114
  rhubarb softserve cheesecake 115

chestnuts
  chestnut hummus 36–7
  Sunday stuffing 70

chicken
  chicken kyiv, hash browns and rainbow
    coleslaw 84–7
  fish (or chicken!) pie 99–101

chicken livers Sunday stuffing 70

chicory salad 19

chocolate 138–9
  100% chocolate pot 141
  DTC's salted caramel chocolate
    rolos 144–5
  hot chocolate tarts 140
  kosher (chocolate) black pudding 147
  light chocolate mousse 146
  the Parlour wagon wheel 135–7
  wafer thin mints 148–50

coleslaw rainbow coleslaw 23

compote, fruit 179

condiments
  aioli 169
  cranberry sauce 92–3
  fruit compote 179
  horseradish 68
  Houses of Parliament sauce 168
  ketchup 168
  mayonnaise 169
  pickles for a picnic 34–5
  salad cream 22
  tartare sauce 169

corn, popped veal chops with creamed,
  sweet and popped corn 74–5

cranberry sauce 92–3
  fried brie with cranberry sauce 88–9

cream
  100% chocolate pot 141
  cheat's vanilla ice cream 180
  crème brûlée tart with too many
    flowers 111
  crème Chantilly 181
  DTC's salted caramel chocolate
    rolos 144–5
  lazy lemon pudding 119
  light chocolate mousse 146
  panna cotta 118

cress potato, egg and cress salad 22

crispbreads almond crispbreads 108

crumble and the Sunday traditions 120–3

crumpets mushroom 'tea' and hot buttered
  crumpets 28–9

curried dishes kitchari – kedgeree 52–4

custard 106
  baked almond custard 108
  crème brûlée tart with too many
    flowers 111
  deep fried custard 109
  eggnog caramel custard 108
  hot custard 109
  Stilton custard with walnuts 46–7

PARLOUR

5 Regent Street

Kensal Green

London NW10 5LG

Proprietors: Mr & Mrs Jesse, Ada & Monty Dunford Wood

Acknowledgements

I would most like to pay homage to my incredibly beautiful, hardworking, understanding, intelligent and patient wife, Mrs Jessie, who sometimes has said the ONLY reason she married me was for my liver pâté (page 33 for those looking to resurrect the flickers of a romantic flame), sadly not 'one' of the reasons...

She has been with me every step of the way from sad to happy, big hope to no hope, from will I or won't I, and some money to no money. Not always necessarily in that order.

We have managed not only to create a lovely pub/restaurant/bar/café/crèche/coffee shop and sometimes even cinema, but we even also made time to make and have twins, Ada and Monty, whose birth also just happened to coincide with the takeover of the business in the same bloody month. Not something I would necessarily recommend to those with a faint heart, nor even those fully fighting fit.

Thank you also to the rest of my family, Mama Emma, Farter Hugh, Rollo, Pasco and Aquila, and in-laws, Omsa, Tim and Uncle Si, who have occasionally been rewarded for their support by my nourishing and sometimes even heart-warming food, and the odd appearance in the family WhatsApp group. I have been rather absent at many weddings, funerals, dinners and days out over the last 20 years, but it might just be about to get a little better. They have provided flower arranging and old man's beard, childcare and road kill, waiters and waitresses, built tables and booths, graffiti'd the toilets, created paintings and designed logos, postcards and beermats, and are even responsible for some dangerously strong (and some may say illegal) banana homebrew that has been seen behind the bar. All courtesy of the family.

There is also the Parlour family, not blood relatives but brethren of another dimension who have all contributed to where we are today. It has not all been plain sailing, and there has been rather too much blood, a lot of sweat and plenty of tears involved in hauling us out of the back streets of NW10 to the very small local pedestal we find ourselves on today.

Some have left a legacy and something that helps make Parlour all the better, then, today and in the future and beyond, and we thank Hamish for his candles, Chris for his Not-in Hill Cocktail, Piotr for his wood effect tool and Sal for her lazy bread.

There have also been some great characters along the way; Kirsten for her never-ending flowers and flat whites, Saydo for his perseverance, Richard K for his dancing, Lowell for his ice-cool consistency, Kamila for her energy, Chilli for her determination, Polona for her sparkle, Guillaume for his accent and Alex Batbold for his unflappable efficiency. Larry the 'apprentice' chef also deserves a mention in helping all of the food in the book to come alive, and even taste great.

We will continue to improve and innovate, continue to serve and entertain. Just wait and see what the next five years has in store...

Publisher Jon Croft

Commissioning Editor Meg Avent

Project Editor Emily North

Art Director Matt Inwood

Assistant Art Director and Designer Marie O'Mara

Assistant Designer Nathan Shellard

Photographer Lauren Mclean
laurenmclean.com

Illustrators Hugh and Jesse Dunford Wood

Food Stylists Jesse Dunford Wood and Parlour team

Recipe Editor Rachel Malig

Proofreader Kate Wanwimolruk

Home Economist Amy Stephenson

Indexer Cathy Heath

This book wouldn't have come to the wider audience without the help of Jon Croft and Meg Avent, who chuckled to my stories in all the right places over a few lunches, and thought writing them all down might make enough for a book. Emily North who has spent many long days and nights putting it all in order and making it happen, Marie O'Mara and Nathan Shellard who have made it look beautiful under the watchful eye of Maestro Matt Inwood. Rachel Malig who edited the recipes with the precision of a mother's watchful eye, and my dear friend Lauren Mclean who has been photographing with me for a few years, and has produced her best work yet on this book.

Thank you for the cross-pollinating support provided by PR maestros Zoe Wilmer and Amy Williams from Samphire, who have helped project me from nowhere to the dizzy heights of London NW10 – and also having a big hand in organising this 'ere book.

Thank you all, Hurrah!

About the author

Jesse Dunford Wood is an inspiring British chef (trying to) making his mark on the London dining scene with his wit and talent for taking classic dishes and reinventing them. Having come to the kitchen in a very round-about way, mostly via art school and long-winded dinner parties, Jesse quickly took the opportunity to work at some of the world's best restaurants, both in the kitchens and also front of house.

Returning to England, Jesse teamed up with Oliver Peyton in 2006 to open restaurants at the National Gallery, which received rave reviews for its familiar and fun, not to mention colourful, take on British food.

Following his adventures and experience, he first opened The Mall Tavern with partners in Notting Hill Gate, where the Cow Pie, Kyiv and Arctic Rolls were all born. He then traded that for full independence, and decided to go out on his own, opening Parlour in 2012 with the support of his incredibly talented family.

Absolute Press
An imprint of Bloomsbury Publishing Plc

50 Bedford Square   1385 Broadway
London   New York
WC1B 3DP   NY 10018
UK   USA

www.bloomsbury.com

ABSOLUTE PRESS and the A. logo
are trademarks of Bloomsbury Publishing Plc

First published 2017

© Jesse Dunford Wood, 2017
Photography © Lauren Mclean, 2017
Image used on pages 6, 7, 12, 13, 104, 105,
166, 167, 182, 183 from horiyan/Shutterstock
(59198521)

Jesse Dunford Wood has asserted his right
under the Copyright, Designs and Patents Act,
1988, to be identified as Author of this work.

British Library Cataloguing-in-Publication Data
A catalogue record for this book is available from the British Library.

Library of Congress Cataloguing-in-Publication data has been
applied for.

ISBN:
HB   9781472938497
ePDF   9781472938510
ePub   9781472938503

2 4 6 8 10 9 7 5 3 1

Printed and bound in China by C & C Offset Printing Co.

Bloomsbury Publishing Plc makes every effort to ensure that the papers used in
the manufacture of our books are natural, recyclable products made from wood
grown in well-managed forests. Our manufacturing processes conform to the
environmental regulations of the country of origin.

To find out more about our authors and books visit www.bloomsbury.com. Here
you will find extracts, author interviews, details of forthcoming events and the
option to sign up for our newsletters.